As I See It

As I See It

My Spiritual Journey

Gregory L. Branch

iUniverse, Inc.
New York Lincoln Shanghai

As I See It
My Spiritual Journey

Copyright © 2007 by Gregory L. Branch

All rights reserved. No part of this book may be used or reproduced by any means, graphic, electronic, or mechanical, including photocopying, recording, taping or by any information storage retrieval system without the written permission of the publisher except in the case of brief quotations embodied in critical articles and reviews.

iUniverse books may be ordered through booksellers or by contacting:

iUniverse
2021 Pine Lake Road, Suite 100
Lincoln, NE 68512
www.iuniverse.com
1-800-Authors (1-800-288-4677)

Because of the dynamic nature of the Internet, any Web addresses or links contained in this book may have changed since publication and may no longer be valid.

The views expressed in this work are solely those of the author and do not necessarily reflect the views of the publisher, and the publisher hereby disclaims any responsibility for them.

Edited by: Anne M. and Gregory L. Branch

ISBN: 978-0-595-44270-6 (pbk)
ISBN: 978-0-595-88600-5 (ebk)

Printed in the United States of America

IN MEMORY
My mother, the late Jessie Lou Pertillar Branch
My father, the late William Harvey Branch
and
My friend, the late Rev. Carl R. Hewitt

Contents

Acknowledgements ix
CHAPTER 1	The Transition	1
CHAPTER 2	My First Spiritual Encounter.	4
CHAPTER 3	The Awakening.	7
CHAPTER 4	Lorna's family	13
CHAPTER 5	Knowledge is Power.	16
CHAPTER 6	The Prophesy	25
CHAPTER 7	My Parents' Families	29
CHAPTER 8	The Power Of Choice	34
CHAPTER 9	Reincarnation	39
CHAPTER 10	Choosing to be Reborn	42
CHAPTER 11	Meet The Branches	46
CHAPTER 12	The Forgotten Prediction	52
CHAPTER 13	The Gift	54
CHAPTER 14	Wisdom From The Past	58
CHAPTER 15	The Essence of Spirit	64
CHAPTER 16	My Ultimate Manifest	71

Chapter 17	Our New Home	79
Chapter 18	A Celebration for Mom	84
Chapter 19	My Parents' Passing	89
Chapter 20	Carl Hewitt's Passing	96
Chapter 21	The Advantages of Spiritual Meditation	99
Chapter 22	The Rhythm of Life	103
Chapter 23	Consider This	106

Back Page Biography..........111
Footprints..........113

Acknowledgements

My lovely wife Anne's unrelenting support and encouragement helped immeasurably in providing me with the confidence necessary to complete this book. Her inspiration has been truly heaven sent. Words alone could never convey how grateful I am to have her by my side. My love for her is infinite.

I dedicate this book to my daughter, Tonia Marie Branch and to my stepdaughters, Tina Marie Von Flatern, Kathleen Marie Guillen, Jacqueline Marie Monteiro, Susan Marie Hardge, and Elizabeth Marie Baptista. I sincerely hope the contents of this book will inspire and motivate them to continually search to find their purpose in life.

The opportunity to know Carl Hewitt has been a blessing exceeding all I could have imagined in this life. Through him, I have enjoyed much of life's abundance. His knowledge of the Gifts of the Spirit and how to access it has been an invaluable asset in my life. I will forever be indebted and grateful to him. He never hesitated to share his wisdom and knowledge of the spirit world. The brilliance of his life will shine eternally.

Throughout this book you will find verses that came to me as I slept. I sincerely believe that they came to me from my mother who is now in spirit world. The inspiration for writing this book came to me from her as well. I feel the poetry she inspired should be shared by all.

Chapter 1

The Transition

After the third series of my doorbell ringing, it was clear that whoever it was at the front door was not going to let themselves in. Expecting my wife Lorna's hospice nurse to arrive at seven that morning, I left the front door unlocked. I assumed that she would let herself in. Frustrated at being disturbed, I flung the front door open. To my surprise it was not the nurse but the welcoming face of my friend Carl Hewitt.

I tried to call him two days before but I only got his answering machine. The message on his answering machine stated that he was out of town and would not be returning for a week. As I welcomed him inside, he explained to me that he sensed the urgency of my voice on the message I left on his answering machine. He immediately decided to end his stay in Washington State and returned to Connecticut. Upon arriving, he drove directly to my home.

Carl Hewitt was a gifted psychic medium who I first met seventeen years earlier. From my first encounter with him, his readings forever changed my viewpoints on life and death. Most of what he predicted happened to me over the next seventeen years. Fear of being considered crazy had prevented me from sharing my initial encounter and subsequent readings with anyone. The fact that his predictions had become reality drew me back to him for readings time and time again.

I explained to Carl that the Director of Hospice of Southeastern Connecticut had contacted me with concerns about my wife Lorna's passing. She suggested I might consider having a religious minister or priest commune with her. She believed that an encounter with a layperson might help her to pass over. I had grown to respect and appreciate Carl's ability to communicate with those of the unseen world and thought he was the right person to contact.

Her nurse's daily report indicated that although my wife's vital signs were at zero, she continued to breath, fighting death as if she was afraid to pass.

The ringing at front door bell was persistent. After letting him in, I escorted Carl back to my wife's bedside and left them alone. Although she was comatose, Carl was able to pick up on her vibration and communed with her for about fifteen minutes. He returned to the room where I was and explained to me in detail that she would pass within twenty-four hours. In touching her vibration, he had learned that she had been afraid to let go, fearing she might end up in Hell. Carl suggested that I get in touch with him after Lorna's passing. He indicated that he would then explain to me in detail the transition of death. Although Lorna's family members were devout Jehovah's Witnesses, she was not. During our marriage of eleven years, we had avoided the efforts of her family to get us to join their church. Because of our choice, we had little association with the family.

She had been diagnosed with Lyomile Sarcoma, a form cancer, only fifteen months earlier. This cancer originated as fibroids in her uterus. A hysterectomy and the removal of her left lung failed to curtail the cancer's spread. Nearing death, she now wondered if that decision destined her to fire and brimstone. While communing with her, Carl reassured her to let go and let God. She passed over twenty-four hours later, on September 3, 1994. Lorna only lived to be forty-six years old.

Two weeks after Lorna passed, I met with Carl as he had suggested. During my very first visit to his office, Carl went into a trance like state. His vibration changed to that of those who had passed on into the unseen. Once in this state, he was able to receive messages from those whom had passed on to the spirit world. While Carl was in trance, Lorna came through. She assured me that she was free of pain and in the company of relatives who had passed before her. She thanked me for being loyal and supportive during our marriage. "To thy own self be true", was her advice to me.

Chapter 2

My First Spiritual Encounter

My first encounter with Carl Hewitt had been seventeen years prior. A friend named Suzanne Steinberg had heard about his ability to see into the future. Since she was unsure and concerned about her future, she made an appointment to see him for a reading. I urged her not to keep the appointment. I scoffed at the idea of anyone seeking a fortuneteller. I believed that they were all crooks and phonies, but she kept the appointment against my better judgment. The reading took place in Carl's office in Chesterfield, Connecticut.

Suzanne was upset with the reading she had gotten from Carl. She found communication through Carl to be quite vague and casual. That which came through in her reading had little to do with her; it was mainly about me. The experience left her feeling as if the reading should have been for me instead of her.

Three hours and eighty miles later, she showed up at my apartment in Worcester, Massachusetts. She urged me to shut up, sit down, and listen to a cassette recording of her reading. The voice on the recording came through with clear diction. He spoke as if he knew me personally. He even knew that I had just shaved off my beard. He also mentioned other personal matters. I felt violated by his knowledge of me.

In an effort to expose his deceit, I made an appointment to see this shyster myself. My appointment was scheduled for three weeks later. Upon meeting Carl Hewitt, I was immediately taken over by his warm and gentile manner. He welcomed me into his office and offered me a seat. He asked me to take off my jewelry and hand it to him. Although I complied with his request, I had great reservations about the necessity of doing so. Sensing my reluctance, he explained that the presence of any metals on the body would interfere with his ability to communicate with Spirit. I later learned that the energy within our body is attracted to any jewelry we might be wearing. By holding that same piece of jewelry, a medium is able to pick up on and read our vibrations. He then recited a prayer asking all that came through his lips be true and positive. After taking a sip of water from a glass, he slumped into at trance.

My first reading through Carl left me angry and frustrated. The idea that anyone could communicate with the dead went against all that I had been taught. Having had been raised as a Baptist, I fully accepted the teachings of that religion. I had been baptized at the Blue Hills Baptist Church in Hartford, Connecticut at the age of fourteen.

I was accustomed to spending almost all day of every Sunday at church. Sunday school, youth fellowship, and the youth choir rounded out my Sundays. I was brought up to believe that knowledge of God through the church and receiving a good education, were necessary ingredients to becoming a success in life.

I spent two weeks during three summers at Camp Wightman in Jewitt City, Connecticut. This camp was owned and supported by the Connecticut Council of Baptist Churches. Building ones' life around the principals of the Baptist religion was the cornerstone of the camp. By the time I entered my junior year in high school, the Baptist ministry was the profession I most admired.

My great grandparents, grandparents and their siblings all lived in a world of devotion to church and family. We believed that following the footsteps of Jesus Christ would insure everlasting salvation and guarantee a ticket into Heaven.

Prior to graduating from high school, I consulted with religious leaders from the major faiths throughout the greater Hartford area. I met with each leader privately asking them all to respond to the same question. Should I pursue the life of a minister or a priest? Their answer of yes, was meaningless as more importantly, I needed to know why. I found none of their answers to be convincing, so I chose a different path.

Chapter 3

The Awakening

When I first met Carl Hewitt, I was working as a sales manager for a chemical company. My accounts were primarily located in Worcester County, Massachusetts. I sold sanitation products to institutional accounts, which covered the gamut from floor cleansers to sanitizers used in surgery. I had graduated from Bloomfield High School in June of 1965. I spent the next two years in college while the Vietnam conflict was intensifying. Our government had instituted a military draft lottery to provide personnel to fight for the cause. I registered with the Selective Services as required by law, but I had no intention of serving. I was against the war. My position fueled my determination to succeed in failing the written portion of the Selective Service Exam. That rejection meant that I could continue with my goal of getting a college education.

I clearly remember sitting next to an obese kid on a bus taking us to the Selective Service Depot in New Haven, Connecticut. This would be his third attempt to pass the physical portion of the entrance exam. His obesity had been the reason for the two previous rejections. He desperately wanted to join the military and serve in Vietnam. His burning desire to serve was contrary to mine. I wished we could have traded places. We sat next to one another on the bus on the return trip back to Hartford after taking the exam. I was quietly elated with my rejection. He was ill and depressed having been rejected once again. However, my elation in being rejected was short lived. I received a written order from the Selective Service Board requiring me to retake the exam in six weeks. Because I was already well into my second year of college, my failing score in the written portion of the exam seemed to be improbable.

My father felt I should make an earnest effort to pass the upcoming exam. With a passing score, I would be able to choose a branch of the military to enlist in. If I were drafted first, I would loose that choice and automatically be assigned to the Army. I subsequently passed the exam and decided to enlist in the Navy. My decision to join the Navy was based on three reasons. The first consideration was that my father had served in the Navy during the World War II. Next, in my way of thinking, was the Navy's reputation for offering excellent educational opportunities. Lastly but not least, there was the possibility of getting to see the world with very little chance of experiencing combat. I enlisted in the U.S Navy in July 1967, serving for six and a half years of active duty. I enrolled in correspondence college courses while I was at sea and studied at local institutions of higher learning when shore duty would allow. I served one tour of duty in Viet Nam, while attached to the USS Kitty Hawk. After returning to the states, I applied to and was accepted into the Navy's Dental School, which was located in San Diego, California. I graduated from that school with the military equivalency of an associate's degree in Dental Technology in 1971. Upon graduation, I was transferred to the U.S. Naval Submarine Base, in Groton, Connecticut. I was attached to the dental clinic there, and served in that capacity for the remainder of my naval career. I received an honorable discharge from the U.S. Navy in November 1973. In December of 1994, I accepted the challenge of an Army Reserve Recruiter by taking and successfully completing a military officer's candidacy entrance examination. I managed to score high enough to qualify for enrollment into this elite leadership program. I attended Officer Candidacy School at the Connecticut Military Academy, in association with the University of New Haven for the next two years. I graduated in May 1976 and earned the commission of Second Lieutenant. The focus of my studies was in the fields of military science and psychology.

    I remained a devout Baptist until 1970. The awakening that forever changed my relationship with the church and religion came to me by mail. While stationed aboard the USS Kitty Hawk, I received a letter from my church reminding me that I was delinquent in paying my tithes. Here I was serving my country during a time of war, while my church back home was only concerned with my tithes. That letter caused me to view the church and religion in a completely different light. I came to the realization that religion was big business. My appreciation for the church immediately changed. Although I still believed in God as our Creator, I no longer believed that membership in a church assured my salvation. In spite of my new attitude towards religion, I still considered psychics and fortunetellers to be demonic. My first encounter and spiritual reading through Carl Hewitt challenged my knowledge and understanding of the Hereafter forever.

Needing to share my initial experience with Carl with someone, I confided in my grandmother on my father's side of the family. She was quite knowledgeable in religious matters. She not only taught Sunday school, but she had also traveled extensively to numerous religious retreats. Her dining room served as a religious library. She spent her life serving the Lord and getting to know him through reading. My relationship with my grandmother had become strained because of her insistent preaching about Jesus. In an effort to improve our relationship, I called my grandmother by phone to let her know that I intended to spend the next Sunday with her.

Of course, she was overjoyed with my intention to spend the day with her. After spending the next Sunday morning in church, we returned to her home and had dinner together. My grandmother was a great baker; her pantry was a haven for goodies. After discussing that morning's sermon, I shared my encounter with Carl Hewitt with her. She did not seem to be surprised as I shared my experience. I then played the cassette recording of my spiritual reading through Carl. She smiled at me with a look of approval regarding my encounter. She reminded me that God works in mysterious ways. She cautioned me not to rush to judgment about God's workings. She pointed out that ancient religions had revered mediums and prophets.

Modern religion she felt had gone to great lengths to discredit genuine mediums and prophets because they were fearful of their power and influence over mankind. She cautioned me to research and question the authenticity of Carl's ability. I left my grandmother's home determined to more adequately acquaint myself with this phenomenon. I spent hours reading all that I could in reference to psychic phenomena. I could not discount the fact that most of what Carl had predicted, had in fact happened.

Earlier, I mentioned that my father's mother, Nana, was a devoted member of the Baptist faith. She was also an avid researcher of many religions. Her wisdom and research allowed her to keep an open mind in matters pertaining to religion. She did not seem to be surprised when I first spoke of my initial encounter with Carl Hewitt. From her experiences, she had learned that, "All things were possible through God."

Even though we were not of Jewish descent, we celebrated Passover on its first day. I'll never forget how we buttered the Motza bread and ceremoniously drank Manischevitz red wine in honor of this traditional Jewish holiday. My grandmother believed that the triumph of the Jewish people deserved recognition.

Christians worldwide traditionally celebrate Easter and Christmas as their most sacred holidays. These two religious holidays have evolved to provide very little religious significance of their origin. Easter parades with egg hunts and Easter bonnets are commonplace.

Christ's resurrection was his triumph over the crucifixion. The purchase and exchange of gifts at Christmas determine for many merchants whether their business year is profitable or not.

Their promotions during this time of the year are relentless. Although there is some question as to the exact date of Jesus the Christ's birth, Christians' worldwide celebrate it on December 25th.

Despite the Crucifixion of Jesus the Christ over 2000 years ago, God continues to send messengers to enlighten us. Daily, our world is graced by the birth of children whose minds are developed much more than ten percent. This allows them to be more receptive to communication, knowledge and wisdom from the world of Spirit. It has been predicted that, "The meek shall inherit the earth."

Chapter 4

Lorna's Family

I would like to formally thank my stepdaughter, Tina Von Flatern, for her unwavering help in caring for her mother during the last three months of her life. The love, care and compassion she provided during those most difficult days was priceless. Tina, who was twenty-seven years old, shared an apartment with a girlfriend. Although she no longer lived with us, she would come by on alternate mornings to provide care for her mother until a Hospice nurse arrived. On many occasions, her grandmother would stop by to lend a helping hand. My wife's mother had buried her only other child, her son, fifteen years earlier. He had been two years younger than Lorna when a brain hemorrhage cut his life short. The wrenching idea of having to now bury her daughter left her severely depressed. She needed to be medicated just to get through each day.

Tina had two younger brothers, Christopher and Steven. By this time, neither one of them lived with us. Chris was two years younger than Tina. Steve, the youngest was four years behind Chris. They seldom visited their mother during her latter days. Her deterioration was too much for them to bear. Lorna's mother felt guilty about the distant relationship she had with her daughter. She regretted that she had allowed her relationship with Jehovah's Witnesses, to come between them. In spite of it, she helped to make Lorna as comfortable as possible and shed many tears to the end.

In honor of Lorna's final request, her first cousin, who was a Jehovah's Witness Minister, presided over the funeral. The anxious relationship between my wife and her relatives made her funeral that was a sad occasion, even worst. Their tears of regret flowed like a river. Tina, her only daughter, put her personal life on hold and cared for her mother to the end. She and her fiancé, Jeff Von Flatern, refrained from setting their wedding date. They married shortly after Lorna passed away.

As I mentioned earlier, Lorna's decision not to join her family's Jehovah Witness congregation made communication between her and her family difficult. The family always felt that she had chosen me rather than them. Lorna's parents divorced shortly after her brother died and both remarried. Her mother and her new husband lived in Westbrook, Connecticut. Her father and his new wife lived near his mother, in New Brunswick, Canada. Lorna's family had migrated to Connecticut from New Brunswick, Canada in the 50's and 60's. In the early summer of 1989, Lorna and I traveled to New Brunswick to spend time with her ailing grandmother. The drive took us about seven hours. She had become quite ill and her condition was terminal.

Lorna's closest aunt, Norma, rode with us. We spent three days in New Brunswick visiting various members of her family. It was like a family reunion and quite festive. On the eve before our return, Lorna's father insisted that he and I share a few beers. After he purchased a case of his favorite draft beer, we drank while he preached to me about the virtues of the Jehovah's Witnesses.

It became apparent that he was set on converting me to his religion. The more we drank and talked, the more convinced I become that his religion was not for me. We both succumbed to the beer at about four in the morning. He seemed defeated by my resistance to becoming a member of his chosen faith.

That was the last time that either of us was approached by her family concerning religion. Her family members seldom made any effort to speak with us from that moment on.

CHAPTER 5

KNOWLEDGE IS POWER

The accuracy and detail of my first reading through Carl caused me to seek him out for a second reading eight months later. His ability to communicate with those in the unseen world completely blew me away. My high school's motto of, "knowledge is power", prompted me to acquaint myself on this subject. I spent much of my spare time reading all that I could on subjects related to metaphysics.

My research and reading on this subject led me to a very important book. It was entitled, *Communication with The Spirit World of God.* Authored by Johannes Greber, it provided me with a basic understand of Carl's gift. This book opened my mind to a new awareness. In this book, Johannes Greber, a devout Catholic priest, gives his account of personal and life changing experiences. It explained in scientific terms that communication between different dimensions of life is possible. The author begins his introduction in this book with a verse, which was taken from a bible of his day, "But these people scoff at anything they do not understand" Jude 1: 10. He ends his introduction siting another verse taken from that same bible, "Call unto me, and I will answer you and show you great and mighty things which you did not know," Jeremiah 33: 3. Part two of the same book, The Laws Governing Spirit Communication with the Material Creation, really got my attention. (It is quite possible that this book is no longer in print) There are numerous publications however, that offer many points of view concerning this understanding. *Finding Enlightment*, published in 1998 by J. Gordon Melton; *The God Within: A Testament Of Vishnu*, published in 1982 by Elwood Babbit and Charles Hapgood; and *The Seven Spiritual Laws Of Relationship*, published in 1998 by Paul Ferrini, are just a few books of reference on this subject. Music has always been helpful in creating the ideal environment for transitioning into the meditative state. Most houses of worship introduce hymns and spirituals as a means to invoke and attract the influence of God.

This practice has been found to be effective throughout generations in attracting positive spiritual influences. *Herban Shamen: Keys To The Inner Sanctum One*, produced by Tracy Kendrick and Courtney Branch, recorded in 2004, is one of many musical recordings which I have found to be helpful in reaching a spiritual frame of thought for meditation. The choice of music for mediation is purely subjective.

There are seven dimensions of life that exist at different vibrations. Mediums, such as Carl, are born with the ability to attune themselves to more than one vibration, hence, they are known as mediums. All humans are born with various gifts and abilities.

Most of mankind is not aware that these dimensions exist. Because we are ignorant of their existence, the concept of being able to change our vibrations through spiritual meditation, which allows us to receive these gifts, is incomprehensible. After Lorna passed, I was urged by Carl to attend a class, which taught the techniques of spiritual meditation. He was the instructor; I was one of twelve beginners in this class. We met at his office in Chesterfield, Connecticut at seven every Wednesday evening.

I quickly learned that those of the spirit world are always present. Because this world exists at a faster vibration than ours, it remains invisible to us unless we possess the gift of clairvoyance. This is the ability to see into other dimensions. Manmade religion teaches us that communication from the unseen world is purely demonic and comes only from the Devil. Fear of this unseen world is responsible for infinite generations of recycled ignorance about this realm. Many people live a life unaware that learning to attune themselves to this unseen world is not only possible but also enlightening. We are taught that by simply acknowledging God during our lifetime we will reap the benefits in the Hereafter.

The Bible acknowledges numerous accounts of individuals who possessed this ability. They are referred to as The Voice, Seers, Prophets, Mediums and the like. Modern religion has gone to great lengths to discredit their existence. Most of us have been taught that the practice of conjuring up spirits is demonic. I took heed of my grandmother's warning to determine the authenticity of Carl's gift.

Through my research, I found out that Carl was an ordained Minister. He founded the Gifts of the Spirit Church on July 7, 1977. It was located in Chesterfield, Connecticut. Constant ridicule and controversy over his psychic abilities from the so-called religious leaders in the area eventually drove him into seclusion. He believed that all humans are born with Gifts from Spirit.

Our endowment of psychic ability comes to us by way of spiritual influence and guidance. This belief, however, is not accepted by most. Carl would always say a prayer before each reading. He would say, "Lord, God of my being, unto the Father within, come forward with your Light, that I might become a Light unto the world. Come forward with your Knowingness, that I might have Knowingness. Come forward with your Wisdom, that I might be Wise." He would then ask, "only that which is good and true, and from the Spirit world of God, be allowed to pass through these lips." He would ask that his body be used as an instrument during that reading to communicate only that which was good and positive. He would then slump into a trance and begin to speak. His entire being would be transformed and taken over by an unseen force. The force or entity that took control of Carl during those readings would always describe themselves as they appeared while they were living in the physical world.

Sometimes they would give theirs names or make reference of a physical attribute they had possessed to make their identity known. Carl explained that there are seven dimensions of life. These dimensions are: Hertizan, Infrared, Visible Light, Ultra Violet, X-Ray, Gamma Ray, & Infinite Unknown. The Light Spectrum of our universe travels through these dimensions.

Although it remains unseen to most, our physical bodies are also surrounded by spiritual bodies. Our minds serve as the control centers for our bodies. It receives and deciphers all incoming information.

Our bodies function through two minds: Binary and Analogical. The Binary mind takes images from our memory banks, combines it with current images, and interprets them. Most people apply this means of thinking in daily life. With Binary mind we tend to 'flip flop' between the images of our past and those of the present. This is known as Living The Image. Binary thinking interferes with spiritual thought. Analogical mind interprets current images. This is known as Living The Now, or In The Now. When the analogical mind is in use, images are received clear and pristine.

Newborns begin life using analogical mind. Spiritual influences such as site and sounds are uninhibited and brilliant. It is at this stage of life that imaginary friends, in imaginary worlds exist. As Binary reasoning is encouraged and considered to be a sign of adult thinking, analogical reasoning, which might reveal 'imaginary' friends is discouraged. This allows doubt to prevail. Analogical mind attracts spiritual influences. In spiritual meditation we learn to focus on The Now. Matter in the physical world exists at the slowest vibration. This vibration is known as Hertizan. Matter in the seventh and fastest vibration is known as the Infinate Unknown. God, the Creator, the All & All, resides at the pinnacle of this vibration. This is where the White Light of Christ Consciousness resides. White light is the most powerful force in our universe. All matter is energy; matter cannot be destroyed, it can only be changed. The acceptance and acknowledgment of the possibility of life's existence at faster vibrations is a matter of consciousness.

In this book, I made mention of there being seven different dimensions of life. Let me be clearer about their existence. The number seven has significant spiritual meaning. It is representative of all that pertains to God, Christ Consciousness, The Creator. I'll name just a few of them. The following references have been taken from the Crystalinks.com/numerology, website: There are seven ages of man (our bodies go through a change every seven years), seven ancient wonders of the world, seven circles of Universe, seven cosmic stages, seven days of the week, seven Heavens, seven Hells, seven pillars of wisdom, seven rays of the sun, seven musical notes. My mother's vanity license plate for her Dodge van was inscribed, JESSI 7. The security system in my parents' home had the numeric combination of 7777. This number was always prominent with our family.

There are seven levels of consciousness. These seven levels are also commonly known as Seals in the body. These Seals, or levels of consciousness, are divided into two major categories. The first three levels, which correspond to the Groin, the Lower Abdomen, and the Solar Plexus, comprise what is known respectfully as Sub-consciousness, Social-consciousness, and Conscious Awareness, or Reality. Starting with the next levels, they correspond with the Thymus, the Thyroid, the Pineal Gland, and lastly the Pituitary Gland. In these areas, Bridge-Consciousness, Super Consciousness, Hyper-Consciousness, and Ultra-Consciousness reside. Focused breathing forces these Seals to open to each level of vibration throughout the human body.

Practicing controlled breathing causes these seals to open. This exercise is known as Consciousness and Energy. Practice of this breathing technique allows us to become more and more successful at speeding up our body's vibration. This allows us to receive communication from higher vibrations. The world's most famous master of this form of meditation was Jesus the Christ; Jesus was his given name. The word or term Christ, which is often misused as his last name, refers to his ability to harness, control and use energy within the universe. His omnipotence has no equal. Endowed with all of the Gifts of the Spirit, he is the foremost master of the Universe.

As we have all been taught, many of his contemplations came through meditation. He lived and gave his physical life on this earth plane. The purpose of his existence on our earth plane was to show mankind, by example, that all things are possible: To Make Known The Unknown. Religious leaders of his time never understood his purpose. They scoffed at and were threatened by his ability to perform what were called miracles. Those miracles were considered to be a threat to the powerful religious leaders of the day.

His crucifixion was their way of destroying his power and influence over multitudes of people. Jesus demonstrated many miracles. He tried in vain to convince mankind that all was possible through the Gifts of the Spirit. He often said, "The things that I do, so too can you." There exist today over eleven hundred different religions throughout the world. Most of the world's major religions teach us that the road to God, must go through mankind's religious leaders.

Most religions insist that only through worship in Churches, Cathedrals, Synagogues, Temples, and Mosques can we hope to know God. This belief has been responsible for the division, destruction, and death of mankind over mankind since the beginning of time. Communication with the Spirit World of God, once understood and practiced, allows for worship and inspiration from our Creator to all living beings, at any time and in any place. Mankind need not be in the company of others to receive the blessings of the spirit. Congregations that gather to meditate often experience manifestations from the Spirit world as their collective efforts invoke the Laws of Attraction.

Personal and direct communion with the Creator remains just a few breaths away. As I indicated early on in this writing, there is scientific evidence, which supports the existence of numerous universes (worlds). It is a fact that their vibrations determine whether their existence is visible to the human eye or not. Communication within these realms is confined to the relative laws and by-laws of nature that apply to that universe. Religion and science have been in disagreement on this subject for far too many years. Scientists who have an understanding of Quantum Physics are familiar with this principle.

Until the worlds of science, physics and religion learn to compromise, understanding the subject of spiritual communication will forever be a mystery to most. Until this bridge of knowledge and understanding is crossed, mankind in general will remain ignorant of the benefits of spiritual communication through meditation. Most of us assume that religious beliefs and concepts that have been passed on to us by family members remains the only effective way to know God. It is assumed that any deviation from these beliefs invites an open invitation to Hell and its inhabitants.

As the laws of nature apply equally, the Law of Attraction determines what entities we can commune with. There are two kinds of dimensions. They are known as kingdoms: one is the Kingdom of God and the other is the Kingdom of Satin. It is wholly important to know this when asking for communication from other dimensions of life. Failure to do so opens oneself up to communication from both the good and evil kingdoms.

The total destruction of the World Trade Centers in New York City by terrorists, is a horrific reminder that absolute power and omnipotence is available to those who unknowingly invoke the Kingdon of Satan.

Chapter 6

The Prophesy

The coming of Jesus the Christ, the Son of God, was prophesied long before he actually existed. He was sent to us by God the Creator to make known, the Unknown.

He was born to Mary, his mother through Devine Intervention. He lived his life on our earth plane as a normal man and demonstrated to us that all things were possible through God. Since the beginning of time, beings have inhabited our earth plane endowed with Gifts of the Spirit. Moses, Mohammed, Krishna, Gandhi, and Buddha are just a few of many masters who have lived among mankind. They all demonstrated Gifts of the Spirit. These masters of the universe were able to assume a meditative state of mind by touching on unseen vibrations of life.

The Hertizan dimension that we live in vibrates at the slowest speed of all dimensions. Masters possessing this knowledge knew how to speed up their vibrations to see ahead or into the future. All masters of the universe possess auras. This white light that surrounds their bodies is a direct result of their ability to harness the energy within our universe. Most spiritual masters applied a principle that is similar to spontaneous combustion to depart our vibration. This method of departure is demonstrated in the movie, *Powder,* produced in 1995, with the leading character played by Sean Patrick Flanery. For far too many generations, religions have created fear of the practice of Consciousness and Energy as means of becoming spiritually enlightened. They often preach that such a practice is an open invitation to the Devil to visit our world. The late Leonardo Da Vincci, Abraham Lincoln, Joan of Arc, The Wright Brothers, Mother Teresa, Martin Luther King, Jr., John Lennon, and Alexander the Great, were living examples of great achievers who made great use of the Gifts of the Spirit.

More modern examples may include Michael Jordan and Tiger Woods. Their achievements and abilities are constant reminders and symbols of possibilities that exist in the human experience. Because we, in general, are ignorant of the Gifts of the Spirit, we hold in awe the achievements and accomplishments of these individuals, both past and present. We fail to recognize and consider the possibility of influence from another dimension.

The combination of moisture and air vibrating at a very slow speed allows for the formation of clouds. The dense concentration of these clouds, at times, prevents us from seeing the sun. But the sun still shines in spite of our inability to see it. Much like the clouds, inhabitants of the Hertizan dimension vibrate at slower speeds than those of other dimensions. This unseen world, like the sun, still exists. As I indicated earlier, all matter is energy, and energy cannot be destroyed.

When we die, the energy of our body remains in an unseen form. The essence of our being, now sped up, continues to exist at a faster vibration in another dimension. The next dimension we move to will be determined by the Laws of Attraction and also by the level of consciousness we reached when we lived in the physical. We, in most cases, will be attracted to like beings that have also passed on. The conscious level we attained when we where alive will have the same power and attraction to us in the Hereafter.

Entities, though not aware that higher dimensions exist, are still governed by the Laws of Attraction and will continue to evolve upward from lower dimensions. These lower dimensions are primarily inhibited by earth bound ghosts and angels. The ultimate purpose of life in the physical world is to evolve. By means of continued evolution, we travel closer and closer to our Creator, which is also known by many as The Godhead. It exists at the pinnacle of the highest dimension, the Infinite Unknown. In this dimension, all is known.

Early in this book I stated that my high school's motto was, "Knowledge is Power." Utilization and respect for the power of Spirit is highly underrated because most humans are unaware of the existence of this dimension. Untold numbers of sincere and devoted worshipers have lost the faith and belief that the power and resources of God's Kingdom are accessible to them. Doubt has weakened the faith of many who yearn to go to Heaven.

By adulthood most humans have little belief that continuing to remain faithful has any spiritual reward. Most people are convinced that they are not deserving of God's mercy. Modern religions have taught us that Sin separates mankind from God. Their doctrines teach that we can only hope to be spared by gaining entry into Heaven, through practicing their religious beliefs.

Furthermore, many religions teach that upon death, we go to Purgatory. There it is decided whether or not we end up in Heaven or in Hell. Once we arrive in Purgatory, judgment is passed on 'the deeds of our life'. I believe that fear of judgment, which is a religious creation, has spiritually enslaved and controlled the masses. God judges no one. No man has the authority to determine who gets into Heaven. Millions have lived and died under this indoctrination. Ironically, only man judges man. Multitudes believe that memorization of spiritual passages from holy books guarantee their entry into the gates of Heaven. Ignorance is bliss. Many have been taught that confession is necessary to have a chance into get to Purgatory. Fear and fear alone, still remains to be the major obstacle in preventing mankind from receiving the Gifts of the Spirit.

CHAPTER 7

▼

My Parents' Families

My mother, Jessie Lou Pertillar Branch, was the second oldest of twenty-one children. Her parents were Charles and Clara Pertillar. My grandfather, Charles Pertillar's mother was a Benyard. Their marriage created the union of these two families. My mother had one older brother named Lawrence Pertillar. There were no sets of twins in the family and each birth was of the opposite gender from the other. My grandmother Clara's, maiden name was Countryman. She was also one of twenty-one children. These three great families were of French, North American Indian, and African origin.

It should come as no surprise that this union between the Pertillar and Benyard families became one of the largest on record in the history of Hartford, Connecticut. The city of Hartford officially recognized this union by a proclamation in 1995. At that time, there were over three hundred members of this family in the grater Hartford area and over fifteen hundred nationally.

This family presently spans the entire United States and Canada. Family reunions are held in Georgia, California, and Connecticut. My grandparents on both sides of the family migrated from the state of Georgia during the early 1900's. It must have been a shock for my father, who was an only child, to marry into such a large family.

Understandably, my childhood experiences in both families were quite different. My grandmother's home on my father's side was usually very quiet. Because there was always some activity going on at my grandmother's home on my mother's side of the family, it was seldom quiet. The most common link between the two families was their devotion to the Baptist religion and reverence for God. I attended numerous Sunday school services with my aunts and uncles. As of this writing, two of my uncles, Cecil Pertillar of Hartford, Connecticut, and Gayhall Pertillar of Harrisburg, P.A., are both practicing Baptist Ministers. One of my aunts, Virginia Pertillar of Hartford, Connecticut is also a practicing Minister. The actions of our daily lives reflected our unquestionable faith and devotion to the church. Our families were thoroughly indoctrinated in the teachings of the Baptist experience.

During my first spiritual reading, the entity that came though identified herself as Hattie. Hattie Crews was my great grandmother on my father's side of the family. She identified herself as "The one who lived across the street from Hopewell Baptist Church in Hartford, Connecticut." She reminded me that she used to chew tobacco. As a child I called her Momma. and I would go to her apartment after school and wait there until my parents came for me. She often sent me across the street to buy her Beechnut chewing tobacco. I remember her spitting into a brass spittoon as she told me many stories. My great grandmother was of Indian (from India) and African decent. Her husband had died many years before I was born. He had been a freed slave who was half African and half Egyptian. He fathered two daughters: my grandmother, Ethel Branch Peterson and my great aunt, Anna B. Anderson; I called her aunt Bee. She and my great grandmother lived together.

My grandmother married Richard Branch and had only one child; my father, William H. Branch.

My father and his mother shared very little with me about my biological grandfather's family. He was the oldest of eight children. My father shared the same name as his grandfather, and his uncle, William Branch Jr. Family records seem to indicate that the Branch family originated from Buena Vista, Georgia around 1912. Although records show them in large numbers in Charleston, South Carolina, and also in Hartford, Connecticut, there are descendants throughout the United States of America. Records also show various spellings of the family name, some ending with apostrophe "e", and others with just the letter "e". They were of French, African and American Indian ancestry.

My grand mother's sister, Anna, married a man with the last name, Anderson. I never knew him. Richard Branch, my grandfather, was killed in a construction accident when my father was fourteen years old. My grandmother later remarried a man named Robert Peterson; we called him Pete. He was a very kind man.

He never hesitated to show me off as his grandson. I'll never forget the day we spent together in New York City; he took me to the Empire State Building. I remember standing on the street and looking up at the tall building that seemed to disappear into the clouds. That same day he took me to see the Brooklyn Dodgers play at Ebbits Field. He often spoke of his desire to take me to Macon, Georgia when he retired from work. That was where he was born and the place he had spent his childhood years. Early on in his teen years, he moved north to Hartford, Connecticut where he lived with relatives. Years later he retired from the Hartford Electric Light Company, where he had worked as a custodian. I fondly remember seeing his retirement picture in the newspaper. He eagerly showed me the gold watch he was awarded; I couldn't have been more proud of him. Our family prepared a feast to honor his most deserved retirement. Shortly after my grandfather retired, my great grandmother died.

Within days of her burial, my grandparents purchased a three family home on Mansfield Avenue in the city of Hartford. My great aunt Bee lived on the first floor; Nana and Pete lived on the second floor. Their plan was to rent out the third floor. After the closing, my grandfather, Pete, bought his first car. It was a brand new white Cadillac sedan. The family was so happy for him. He and my grandmother, Nana, could now travel and see the country in style.

I remember my grandfather calling the Department of Motor Vehicles to make an appointment for him to take his drivers' exam. Since he had never owned a car before, there had been no need to have a driver's license. I felt that getting his drivers license at the age of sixty-five was pretty cool and well over do. I, at the age of seventeen, already had mine.

Unfortunately, my grandfather never got to drive his new Cadillac. He was diagnosed with sugar diabetes shortly after purchasing his new car. The onset of gangrene led to the amputation of his left leg from the knee down. Six months after that surgery, he died. We, the family believed he died from a broken heart. I believe he simply lost the will to live.

Chapter 8

The Power Of Choice

My great grandmother, Momma, was only one of my deceased relatives who identified themselves' as being present during many spiritual readings I received through Carl Hewitt. They had all passed on long before my time. The identity of many of my deceased relatives often required confirmation by my parents and other older members of the family.

Mankind's greatest power is the power of choice. This power continues to exist even after we pass over. I made mention earlier in this book of a few notable personalities. Their gifts, as I view them, may not be the most obvious ones. There's no doubt that Tiger Woods is the best golfer in the world today; he may in fact be the best golfer ever. It is not unrealistic to consider that he might be host to a master golfer from a different dimension. Tiger's gift to mankind, in my opinion, lies in his ability to raise the bar in his sport in a manner that has raised everyone's expectations in life and it's many challenges. His success is a living testament that reminds us that perfection is possible by all races and to all genders.

Michael Jordan always wanted to have the basketball when winning the game was on the line. His presence of mind and his confidence allowed him to take control of the game with winning results. Mother Teresa's care and devotion to the sick and impoverished was a gift, by example, of humility. The Wright brothers showed us that human flight was possible even though it was believed to be impossible. John Lennon simply asked us to believe.

The words and deeds of Dr. Martin Luther King, Jr. reminded us that all men are created equal and that we all deserve equal treatment. Joan of Arc, through Divine Intervention showed the male leaders of her time that women also possessed the ability to lead. Leonardo DaVincci's brilliant inventions helped to improve the world and inspired mankind to improve his lot.

Alexander the Great did more than just conquer cities; he also improved the circumstances of those that he and his armies conquered. Abe Lincoln changed the consciousness of whites towards blacks in the eighteen hundreds by abolishing slavery. I do not believe that these individuals acted purely alone. I'm convinced that they were used as Instruments of the Spirit world.

It has been stated that the average person uses only ten percent of his mind. Access to the world of Spirit can be gained through the practice of spiritual meditation. Utilization of the remaining ninety percent of our minds may facilitate entry into this realm. Many newborns enter our world daily with more than ten percent of their minds functioning. We often label many of them as Geniuses. They seem to enter our world with knowledge and abilities that are beyond explanation. It is important to consider that their abilities are Gifts from Spirit. The practice of Consciousness and Energy facilitates the opening of ones mind to receive the Gifts of the Spirit from the higher realms of life. This practice allows the remaining ninety percent of our minds to be tapped and utilized.

The practice of Consciousness and Energy in spiritual meditation differentiates spiritual meditation from other types of meditation. This Work, as it is known, requires disciplined repetitive practice. When it is done properly, one feels lightheaded; the result is hyperventilation. When the body becomes hyperventilated, it becomes warm and gives off heat. Practitioners, when meditating outdoors in cold temperatures, have been known to increase their body temperatures so high as to melt snow located in close proximity to them. For best results, one should cover their eyes to keep out all light.

The absence of light combined with repetitive breathing reduces the psychological effect of the earth's gravitational pull. This loss of familiar surroundings facilitates a sensation of floating. For the best results, one should sit in the lotus position insuring that the spinal cord is straight. This alignment improves the attraction of spiritual energy from the unseen world through the central nervous system. The absence of light heightens the responsiveness of the remaining senses in the body. People who are blind rely on other senses in their bodies to compensate for their absence of sight.

Not only do other dimensions vibrate at a faster speed than ours, time within them is also immeasurable. Communication from the unseen world is timeless. Time, as we know it, only has meaning in our dimension. It is not advisable to use our concept of time to measure predictions that come from other dimensions.

BLESSED

I was blessed, as we all are from birth
Blessed in this incarnation with a curiosity for knowledge
and wisdom from the unseen
As all that glitters is not gold
All that we see is not genuine

Chapter 9

▼

Reincarnation

I think it should be noted at this point in this writing, that I believe in reincarnation. I am well aware that my belief is an unpopular one. I am of the opinion that we knowingly make the choice to reincarnate. We choose to make this journey to discover our purpose. I am convinced that we are all destined to make a positive contribution to the world. I don't think that it is necessary for us to always lead by example. The executive branch of our government has been using this ill-fated ideology to justify an increase in our military presence in the Iraq war. It is more important to live by example. To that end, I am convinced that my purpose in this life is to encourage the practice of spiritual meditation. Communication from Spirit has given me more than sufficient proof of my position. I find it hard to believe that God, our Creator, would allow death of the human body to be all that there is. The coagulated energy of our physical existence upon death simply remains in an unseen form. Mankind, has since the beginning of recorded history, taken full credit for its' achievements and accomplishments. I sincerely believe that Spirit has provided man with unseen assistance in improving life's circumstances since the beginning of time. Worship of material things, without reverence to God, ultimately leaves one open to pain and agony in life. Mankind's greed and hunger for power and control over all life on our planet will ultimately lead to our demise. The result inevitability will be experienced directly or indirectly by our offspring. Because mankind is born into the physical world with amnesia of a past existence, we enter this life with no memory of previous lives.

Many of us have had multiple past lives. According to Spirit, I have had three previous lives with my last one ending in 1929. That life was cut short from fatal injuries in an auto accident. Spirit indicated that I was born into this lifetime with the awareness and understanding in alignment with the fourth dimension of life. Each lifetime evolves from a lower to a higher dimension. This is a continuous journey to reach the highest dimension, the Infinite Unknown, at its pinnacle is the Godhead.

The writing of this book was interrupted when I received word of a family tragedy. My wife and I were stunted when we received a call notifying us that Christopher Reed Loukas, Lorna's oldest son, at the young age of thirty-seven, had passed away as a result of a brain aneurysm. His passing was a terrible loss to family and friends alike. His only uncle and one of his great grandfather's also succumbed to the very same illness.

This weakness in blood vessels within the brain appears to be a hereditary condition.

Chapter 10

Choosing to be Reborn

As the Law of Attraction has no limitation, our human traits are passed on to us through heredity. For this reason, newborns quite often resemble their biological parents. Often, the eyes of a host will resemble those of a relative that has passed on. Hence, "the eyes have it", is an expression that is familiar to many. As I said earlier in this book, man's greatest power is the power of choice. The power of choice remains constant even in other dimensions. If an entity chooses to reincarnate and return to this dimension, it must find a host human body to live in. To accomplish this feat, a Spirit must lower its vibration to that of our dimension. Spiritual bodies are made of ectoplasm. Human bodies are made of protoplasm. In accordance with the Laws of Attraction, a Spirit being chooses an unborn child as a host. Most often, Spirits choose a relative to be that host. Spirit enters a mother's body through her womb penetrating the fertilized egg, and is born again. That child usually takes on the physical traits of the biological parents. Most other tendencies are that of the Spirit. For this reason, siblings often have totally different personalities. In many, but not all instances, heredity and family ties are the most overwhelming forms of attraction to Spirits. Reincarnation back through family members is most common. A Spirit's choice to reincarnate is influenced by an overwhelming desire to live again, gaining another opportunity to spiral upwards towards the highest dimension, the Infinite Unknown. After a human being dies and passes over, their actions towards mankind during their previous lifetime will determine their position in the next dimension. The choice to reincarnate gives that Spirit the opportunity to improve their position on the spiral by living a new life with experiences that improve their respect and understanding of mankind in general.

The ego of mankind has overshadowed this idea. We, as humans, assume that all great accomplishments are of our own doing. This ill-fated, self-absorbed attitude has resulted in mankind's lack of respect for man as well as the destruction of our environment.

Sylvester Stone, the leader of the American Rock Band, Sly and the Family Stone, explains the reality of siblings with different personalities in his hit recording, *It's A Family Affair*. Most mediums of our world are beings who in previous lives were greatly attracted to the unseen side of life. Having made the choice to reincarnate, these beings often return to this dimension with medium-like abilities. Manmade religions have gone to great lengths to discredit their validity.

Many people who possess the genuine gift of mediumship have been outcast or destroyed. Most religions, even when their prophecies proved them to be correct, usually found ways to explain away the mystique of their abilities to predict the future. It is written and generally accepted that Jesus, the Christ, went away and meditated for forty days and forty nights. It is generally misunderstood exactly what he did during this period of time. Most people have a very vague understanding of why Jesus, God's only begotten son, came to this world. Mankind had begun to worship and believe that idols possessed the power of God. He sent us Jesus, through Immaculate Conception, to free us from ignorance.

Through Jesus' life we were given the ultimate gift from God and his Kingdom. Incredible power also lies in the Kingdom of Satan. The knowledge of how to tap into the resources of either kingdom is quite powerful. Many of today's Christian followers are ignorant of or have forgotten God's motivation in sending us his son.

Mankind had become devout worshipers of graven images and idols. As God would have no gods before him, Jesus' purpose on this earth plane was to enlighten mankind concerning the Gifts of the Spirit. The cross has become a symbol of Christianity, which adorns most places of worship. This symbol has different meanings to people throughout the world. To some, it is a sign that they are followers of the Christian faith. To others, it is merely worn as jewelry. The cross may or may not have any religious meaning to it. Christian crusaders of past centuries would use the handle of their swords, which was a symbol of the cross, to identify themselves.

One might be run through with the other end of that very same sword if they did not acknowledge Jesus as their lord and savior. Many people stated that they were followers of Jesus so that their lives would be spared. Today, people commonly identify themselves as being devout followers of Jesus when they are threatened with adverse situations. Mankind's casual relationship with God and his "only when it suits me" attitude may be a primary reason why we have not been greater beneficiaries of the Gifts of Spirit.

The Laws of Attraction apply in every dimension. The attractions of the physical world remain after we lay down our bodies and pass over into other dimensions. Sight, one of our most precious senses, is replaced with emotion in the unseen world.

Chapter 11

Meet The Branches

I was the first born of five children to my parents, William Harvey and Jessie Lou Branch. I have three younger brothers, Randall, Courtney, and Terrell; we are all five years apart. I have one sister, Tamara, who is two years younger than my youngest brother. We could not have had two better parents as role models. I was born on August 18, 1947. My father and mother were twenty-one and twenty years old respectively at the time of my birth.

As a child, I did not fully appreciate my good fortune in having them as parents; I assumed that all parents were like mine. Only after joining the Navy did I fully appreciate the rarity of being blessed with their love, patience, and wisdom.

The late Harry S. Truman, the thirtieth President of the United States, spoke of his vision for the country and called it, The New Deal. He became known as the President who, walked softly and carried a big stick. He led the United States and the world with power and authority. My father exemplified that attitude in leading our family. His wisdom and strength of character were two of the many attributes I most admired in him. Respect for elders, devotion to family, integrity, confidence in one's self, pride and discipline, were some of the fundamental principles that he instilled in us. He worked as a civil engineer for the Metropolitan District Commission Water Bureau in Hartford, Connecticut. He was one of the first African American civil engineers to be employed by the agency.

After thirty-seven years of service, he retired in 1991. My siblings and I were also blessed with having the world's greatest mother. Her parents named her Jessie Lou, after one of her deceased relatives. She radiated love and grace; her magnetism was infectious to all who met her. She always taught us by example to respect people from all walks of life. She stressed getting a good education and reverence for God.

Her confidence and persistence in overcoming obstacles was remarkable. Diagnosed with tuberculosis at eleven years old, she spent a year in a sanitarium. After receiving a clean bill of health, she returned home and continued to help her mother raise her brothers and sisters. Returning to school, she eventually graduated on time with her peers from Weaver High School in Hartford, Connecticut in 1945. She furthered her education by graduating from the Academy of Hairdressing and Cosmetology, in that city.

After seeing me through my high school graduation in 1965 and insuring that my siblings were all settled in school, my mother enrolled in and graduated from the State of Connecticut's first class of Para Professionals. She earned her certification in this field of study in 1969. After working in that capacity for only four months, she was diagnosed with Multiple Sclerosis. In spite of the diagnosis, she worked for the next thirty-eight years as a beacon for education in her community.

The town of Bloomfield's Board of Education should be eternally indebted to my mother for her dedication. Her devotion to enriching the lives and minds of the young people is unprecedented. Oddly enough, the interaction between my mother and the youth of her community exemplifies the validity of the Laws of Attraction. She and her students mutually benefited from their exchange of positive energy. While the students were enriched by her passion to teach, she sincerely believed their positive energy helped to promote her well-being. Accordingly, her disease remained in remission for many years. This exchange of positive energy allowed my mother to continue to work; she never retired.

I'll never forget the events of my fourteenth birthday. My dad drove me to Bradley airport, which is located about seven miles north of where we lived in Bloomfield, Connecticut. It was my first visit to an airport. I watched the airplanes land and take off with amazement. While we were there, my dad directed my attention to the huge signs in the terminal. One of them read Arrivals and the other read Departures. He explained to me that although these signs gave directions in the terminal, their symbolism also applied in human characterization.

His explanation was that, when a person acted as if they had 'arrived', they were really 'departing', in the eyes of God. "No one person is any better than another," he said. "Always think well of yourself and hold your head up high". I never forgot what he said. Five years later I found myself preparing to leave home, headed for boot camp in the U.S. Navy. Again, my dad shared a bit of wisdom with me. "Opinions are like assholes," he said, "everyone has one." That understanding has been helpful to me in dealing with many people over my lifetime.

My mother also nurtured me with many words of wisdom. Her explanation of Jesus' love is a treasure. She believed it was impossible to love someone, else unless we first love ourselves. She believed that Jesus always looked for the good in a person. "We may not like everyone we meet," she would say, "but if we look for the good in them we can learn to love them." "Everyone deserves to be understood," she used to say. Misunderstandings between one another have led to the demise of multitudes. My mother would also say, "We never get a second chance to make a first impression. Always make your first encounter with someone memorable."

The year was 1978. During my second spiritual reading through Carl Hewitt, the topic of my first marriage, which had ended in divorce two years prior, was addressed. In September of 1970, I married Judith Val-Marie Angus of Westminster, British Columbia, Canada. Her mother was born and raised in Poland, and her father was of Western Canadian Indian decent. On December seventh the same year, she gave birth to our lovely daughter, Tonia Marie.

Although Judith and I were passionately in love, we had no prior plans to marry. We lived for the moments we spent together. The impending birth of a child being born to unwed parents was out of the question. My parents had always instilled in me the idea that I was responsible for my actions and that I should be held accountable. I however, at the age of twenty-three, lacked the maturity to lead a family. I had no plans to get married before I was twenty-six. Judith, although she was only eighteen years old, was more mature and fully accepted the vows we took on our wedding day. I had just returned from a distinguished tour in Viet Nam, with the Navy. I had also enjoyed limited success as an entertainer. Temptations from outside my marriage proved to be more than I could resist.

Although I loved Judith more than any other woman, I loved myself more. Being immature and selfish, I put my desires first. After five and half years, our marriage ended in divorce.

Our daughter, Tonia Marie Branch, was an angel in every respect. From the moment she entered this world, it was quite apparent that she was a special gift from God. She seemed to glow with a magnetism that was irresistible.

The Spirits that spoke through Carl, reminded me of the guilt of my infidelity. The gift of Tonia increased my feelings of guilt and caused me to feel unworthy of such a blessing. Spirit eased my self-imposed burden by explaining to me that I had indeed gotten married too young. Spirit did not, however, excuse my infidelity. Spirit explained that my actions, as well as all of our actions, are motivated by an irresistible desire for new experiences.

Passing judgment on one another's actions is a human trait. Spirit explained that God judges no one. He simply observes everything. Self imposed guilt and criticism of others has led to the undoing and demise of untold generations. This trait has plagued mankind since the beginning of his existence. Spirit also explained the importance of living in the present. We cannot change the past or alter the future; the present is the only reality we can control.

Words alone cannot convey the respect and admiration I have for Tonia's mother. She did not let the demise of our relationship deter her from providing a good environment for our daughter. She remarried and continued to excel in life. After high school, our daughter graduated from and received a BS in Merchandising from the University of Connecticut in 1992. Today, Tonia Marie is a beautiful, well-adjusted single professional living in Los Angeles, California. My family also deserves credit for guiding Tonia's development from childhood to womanhood. They all contributed to instilling positive values in her.

Chapter 12

The Forgotten Prediction

During the spring of 1980, I again sat with Carl Hewitt for a spiritual reading. I was reminded that the guilt of my actions, which led to a failed marriage, had continued to affect my relationships with other women. It was revealed to me that I would eventually fall in love again and remarry. Spirit predicted that I would cross the path of a woman whose encounter might be life changing. She would have been born in a foreign country on an island. Her skin complexion would be lighter than mine, but she would not be Caucasian. She would have brown hair, be short in stature, very attractive, with a radiant smile. The last two digits in of her birth year when totaled, would equal the number seven. Her personality though different from mine, would create a balance in our relationship. Although our meeting would appear to happen by chance, it would not be. Our encounter would be the result of advanced planning from the world of Spirit. I was warned in advanced not to overlook this opportunity.

Two years later, I met Lorna Lukas and fell in love. The time that passed since that reading caused me to forget about the prediction Spirit had made. After all, I reasoned, it was only a prediction.

During another spiritual reading through Carl Hewitt in 1996, I was told that I would purchase land that would be situated on a river. The banks of the river would be laden with mountain laurel. Because I had no inclination toward purchasing land at that time in my life, the thought of purchasing land anywhere, at any price, seemed to me to be preposterous. During that same reading it was predicted that I would purchase this land with my wife. Since I was at that time a widower, the mere idea seemed to be quite a stretch. I mentally filed the prediction it away.

Confident that Lorna and I were right for one another, we got married on September of 1983. Our wedding ceremony, though small, was a joyous occasion.

Chapter 13

The Gift

During a previous reading I was asked by Spirit when I intended to move back to Connecticut. Since I had no intention of ever moving back to Connecticut, my response to the question was, "never." Spirit disagreed and predicted that I would move back. Spirit believed that I would eventually reside within two miles of Carl Hewitt's office. I considered the prediction to be absurd.

In September of 1983, Lorna and I purchased a home in Oakdale, Connecticut. Oakdale was located eight miles north of our previous home in Old Lyme. Seven miles to the east was the city of New London. I worked there at Girard Toyota/ BMW of New London as an automobile salesman. One day in May of 1985, I found myself sitting in traffic in front of Carl Hewitt's office. While sitting there, I remembered Spirit's prediction of 18 years prior. It suddenly occurred to me that Lorna and I lived quite close to Carl's office. With that thought, I decided to measure the distance to our house from that intersection. It blew me away to realize that the distance was exactly two miles. How could the Spirit have known? During another spiritual reading in 1991, I was asked if I had ever received a ring as a gift; I had not.

Spirit predicted that I would and that it would come from an appreciative client. I started working for Girard Toyota/BMW of New London in 1983. By 1986, my sole focus and goal was to become a successful BMW salesman to the residents of Southeastern Connecticut and Southwestern Rhode Island.

It was there that I had the distinct pleasure of meeting Mr. and Mrs. Edwin Widodo, an Indonesian couple. Their daughter, Christina, had begun attending a local college near the dealership in January 1992. Christina was a student in that city at Connecticut College from January 1992 through May 1994. During those years, Christina's choice of vehicle was BMW. Christina's only sibling Andrew, who was one year behind her, attended Carnegie Mellon University in Pittsburgh, Pennsylvania. What began purely as a business relationship, quickly developed into a friendship.

Our conversations often times had little to do with BMWs. Shortly after meeting the family, I learned that they designed and produced fine gold jewelry. Their company, Christian Diamond Jewelry, which was located in Jakarta, Indonesia, produced one of a kind jewelry for clients throughout the world. In August 1993, they paid me a visit at the dealership.

While they visited, Mrs. Widodo asked my opinion of a ring she had made for the wife of Sweden's Vice President. She had planned to personally go to Sweden to present it to her on the following day. She had developed the habit of wearing any jewelry she made before it was delivered. If it did not look or feel right, she would scrap it and begin again. She was, to say the least, a perfectionist at her craft. The ring was magnificent; it was laden with sapphires and diamonds. I simply remarked that it would surely be treasured.

On Christmas Eve day that same year, Mr. and Mrs. Widodo paid me a surprise visit. I was lost for words when Mrs. Widodo handed me a small box and said, "Merry Christmas." It's contents left me speechless. With sixteen diamonds surrounding a large blue sapphire, it was the most stunning ring I had ever seen. "I can't except this," I said.

"I'll only take it back if you don't like it," she replied. She went on to explain how grateful she and her husband were for my attending to their daughter's automobile needs. Although the service I provided was inconsequential to me, they found it to be comforting and beyond their expectations. I now wear this beautiful ring with everlasting pride. Once again, a prediction from the Spirit came true.

IN GOD WE TRUST

We all possess brilliance within
Controlled breathing brings to light that which is dim
Waste no more of your seven's praying up to heaven
God's abide is on the inside
Through focused meditation, one can elevate their vibrations
To a level that attracts "Masters" of knowledge & wisdom
"To thy own self be true" so your mission in life
And your gifts might be revealed
"God's" abide is on the inside
"God's" abide is on the inside

Chapter 14

Wisdom From The Past

In the spring of 1996, at the recommendation of Carl Hewitt, I attended a five-day spiritual retreat, which was held in Yelm, Washington. This retreat was known as Ramtha's School of Enlightenment. World-renowned experts in the fields of metaphysics gave numerous lectures in classes which often lasted ten hours a day. Here is a listing of some of the topics that were discussed: The Nature of Consciousness and Energy, What is the Soul, Reincarnation, The study of the Human brain & Brain Chemistry, Remote Viewing, and Manifesting from Nothing. These classes were offered for over fifty weeks a year.

I was one of approximately fifteen hundred people in attendance who gathered there from around the planet. I remember meeting people from as far away as Australia, New Zealand, Indonesia, India, and Italy.

As students of spiritual meditation, we gathered at a ranch owned by J. Z. Knight. J. Z. Knight led a very common life as a wife, and as a mother to their children. One day an entity or ghost, as we mortals might call it, materialized in front of her in her kitchen. J. Z. was stunted by this phenomenon. Doubting the experience, she believed it was a figment of her imagination. The following day, this entity appeared before her again. It spoke and introduced itself as Ramtha. This entity claimed to be J. Z's father from a previous life. He announced that his life had ended thirty-five thousand years before. In total disbelief, J Z. completely rejected what she was seeing and hearing. Believing she had lost her mind, she felt she was destined to end up in a mental institution. Fearing criticism, she made no mention of these experiences to anyone. She could only hope that there would be no repeat of this occurrence.

Days later, the entity again materialized in her presence. This time the entity asked for permission to use her body to host his reincarnation. He explained that his desire and purpose in doing so was to enlighten mankind about the working of Spirit. With her approval, she and her body would be used as the "instrument", which would allow him to exist on this earth plane. The transformation would require the energy from J. Z's body to accomplish this feat. This transformation would suspend J. Z's existence, as she knew it, while Ramtha occupied her body. Ramtha convinced J. Z. Knight of his supernatural abilities by bringing to light some of her deepest secrets. He demonstrated feats, which could only be conceived and accomplished by someone with super human abilities.

Finally convinced, J. Z. consulted with her family about this most preposterous proposition. Ramtha promised that he would return J. Z's body back to her, in its original state, when his mission was completed. He also promised J.Z's direct entry into the Infinite Unknown the moment she passed over to Spirit. I fully understand that this entire subject may seem to be far fetched. However, this exchange of energy between mankind and Spirit is not an uncommon phenomenon.

Many of the great and unbelievable wonders of our world have occurred by this very process. Convinced of Ramtha's intension, J. Z. agreed to allow the process of transformation to begin. Ramtha thoroughly explained this conversion process to J.Z. Because J. Z. Knight was a woman, this transformation was not an easy one.

Two thousand years before, Jesus' radical messages and magical demonstrations of the power of Spirit, were considered blasphemy and a threat to those in power. Jesus claimed to be the Son of God incarnated in human flesh. He proclaimed that He had been sent down to earth to enlighten mankind. Although Jesus' claim was considered to be delusional, the leaders of that time considered his growing popularity to be a threat to their power and influence. He was, thusly, eliminated by crucifixion. By using his daughter, J. Z's body as the host, Ramtha gained another opportunity to enlighten us. Disguised in J. Z.'s body, he believed he would be perceived as less of a threat to the powerful.

The coming of the entity, Jesus the Christ, was prophesied long before it actually occurred. The Three Wisemen followed a North Star to find the birthplace of Jesus. That prophecy, having been fulfilled was in part the reason J. Z. Knight allowed Ramtha to use her body. By the time I registered to attend

Ramtha's School of Enlightenment, Ramtha's claim of being reincarnated had spread throughout the world.

Death threats required that J. Z. Knight's relatives be protected by security at all times. There were many attempts to silence Ramtha. Security preparations for Ramtha's worldwide lectures proved to be quite formidable and too expensive; they were eventually terminated.

These retreats, like the four that I attended through 1998, were all held on J.Z. Knight's property amid high security. Ramtha allowed himself to be questioned and tested by world-renowned experts in the fields of parapsychology and science on more than one occasion. The results of their testing was documented and made public to the world. The results concluded that Ramtha was in fact, The Real Deal. The experience of these spiritual retreats has enlightened me and forever changed my beliefs and understanding in God, as our Creator. I completely believe in the power and existence of Spirit.

Manmade religion has gone to incomprehensible lengths to convince us that any so-called communication from the world of Spirit is demonic. The influence of religion on national and corporate powers of the world is undeniable. A prime example of this fact can be seen on U. S. tender. "In God We Trust," is inscribed on all our currency. In spite of this fact, investment in research and development to bring about awareness, understanding and enlightenment of spiritual matters, remains to this day to be virtually non-existent.

The mere idea that a more powerful force than mankind might exist is considered to be a challenge, which threatens control of the masses. Instead, generations of recycled ignorance prevail regarding communication between the visible and invisible spheres of existence.

Many a person or business has been drawn to the allure of money and financial success. The greedy never hesitate to pray for financial windfalls. They wrongly blame God if their dream of a windfall does not occur.

Those who don't have it in abundance believe that acquiring it will provide them with eternal happiness. Ironically, many of the worlds' wealthy end up spending a vast portion of their holdings in an effort to keep what they have acquired. Conversely, many benevolent philanthropists, by sharing their wealth enjoy infinite returns on their investments.

BELIEVE

I don't expect you to understand
But I've conceived and so believe
That by manmade religion
We've been deceived
Realization of God's promise ... be honest
Takes a journey inside
In harmony with nature
To dispel all lies
Don't be ignorant for answers ... be wise
God's love and wisdom comes from within
Transformation through meditation brings us to him

Chapter 15

The Essence of Spirit

During a spiritual reading from Carl Hewitt in 1986, I was given a brief education on some of the principals of the Spirit World. Because most people lack an understanding of these basic principles, it is not surprising to find that the existence of Spirit remains a mystery to most. Consider the following: matter is energy and cannot be destroyed. This energy is the Life Force of all living beings. This Life Force was originally known as Odic Force. This power current to the human body is also known as Vital Force. Today most medical doctors use Vital Statistics to evaluate our state of health. G, which is the seventh letter in the English alphabet, is also a unit of force equal to the gravity exerted on a body at rest. This letter, when it is placed in front of the word 'od', forms the term we know as God. The Creator possesses the greatest concentration of this energy.

Devine inspiration should be taken more seriously than it currently is. Formal education provides us with a vast understanding of the physical world. I'm of the opinion, however, that in general manmade education teaches us what to think, but not how to think.

Consequently, we remain ignorant of the Gifts Of Spirit. Many religions base their origins on what is written in the Holy Bible. Many of them never take into account that virtually all bibles, through translation, have lost their original meaning. The change of one word can alter their entire context.

Many bibles were rewritten to benefit those who commissioned and authored their rewriting. Hence, the King James Version is exactly that, King James' version. I'm not suggesting that his or any version is less than accurate. I'm definitely not an authority on the subject. However, religious indoctrination has led most to believe that all bibles read the same. Believing that their contents are original leaves no one to question their authenticity. Again, ignorance is bliss.

Multitudes have lived, worshiped, and died, ill informed of the most effective means of communication with our Creator. Manmade religions have convinced well-intentioned and devout worshipers that the rewards of this physical life can only be experienced after passing over into the Hereafter. This is not the case. Education and a clear understanding of the principles of communication with the Spirit world are available to all.

Manifestations of Spirit beings such as Ramtha are not uncommon. The exchange of energy between our dimension and a higher one is necessary to bring about manifestations. This spiritual energy conversion most often happens in a confined area. This confined area was referred to as a cabinet in ancient times. Any confined area could be used as a cabinet. A medium would sit in this cabinet and allow Spirits to draw the energy, (OD) from their bodies. That energy would then coagulate. This coagulated energy, which was known as ectoplasm allowed that Spirit's body to become visible. An observer would see this spiritual entity as a ghost or an angel. Spirit would use the medium's voice box for verbal communication. The process of depleting vast amounts of energy from the medium would cause him to appear to be lifeless. The lifespan of most Mediums are often shortened as this transition constantly drains their bodies of life sustaining energy.

Most churches were constructed with what is commonly called a belfry. Belfries of ancient churches were used as cabinets where the collection of ectoplasm took place. Back in the day, they were closed in on all four sides. Often, entry into these cabinets was by way of a staircase, which was usually located in the floor.

These events became known as séances. Manmade religions were effective in inaccurately labeling these occurrences as demonic. These belfries were eventually left open on all sides and constructed to accommodate bells. In more modern times these bells were rung to call the community to worship. Today the Holy Cross, the steeple, and the belfry are considered commonplace in the construction of most churches. Most people are not aware of the original use of belfries in their churches.

Those having the gift of clairvoyance would see these forms as ghosts or angels. Mediums who possessed second sight would recognize the appearance of these Spirits as ghosts or angels. Mediums, as they are called, are sensitive to differing vibrations that occur between dimensions. Clairvoyance is the most commonly known ability possessed by mediums. Clairvoyants have the ability to see what remains unseen to most of us. This Gift is known as having second site. Clairaudience, which is the ability to hear sounds or language when there is apparent silence and Clairsentience, which is super-sensitivity to surroundings, are two lesser known abilities a medium might possess. A medium possessing the gift of clairsentience can usually translate ancient or foreign tongues, bringing the listener to an understanding of the message. All mediums, and there are many types, possess at least one of these gifts. Few possess all. Carl Hewitt possessed all these abilities. The gift of mediumship often runs through families and usually surfaces in every other generation.

Rarely are these abilities as obvious in a person as they were in Carl. By the time he was old enough to speak, it was apparent that he saw and heard things that others around him did not. These abnormalities led to numerous examinations and opinions my medical and psychological experts in the area of North Carolina where he was raised. He was ostracized by most members of his family. The people of his community considered him to be a freak of nature possessed by the Devil. At the young age of 5 years old in 1933, he submitted to a battery of tests to analyze his rare abilities. These tests were conducted at the Dr. Rhines's Institute in association with Duke University in Durham, North Carolina. The results only confirmed what his family already knew. He was indeed a phenomenon.

As a young adult, he was duped into allowing his life story to be chronicled into a movie. Empty promises were made concerning how his life would be portrayed on the big screen. To say the least, he was unhappy with the final production. Some of his remarkable abilities are showcased in this movie titled,

The Gifted One. The movie was made for the National Broadcasting Company and produced by Howard W. Koch, Jr., in 1989.

Being a very humble man, Carl made no mention of this movie to me until 1997. However, he allowed it to be shown one evening during a meditation class I attended. Humility appears to be a common trait shared by most gifted people. They seem to have a special reverence for God, the Creator.

Jesus, the Christ, was also most humble about his gifts and abilities. It is written that whenever he was asked how he accomplished his great feats, he would simply respond by saying, "I am." He made it clear that he did not dwell on the past or live for the future. He lived life in the present.

I find it quite interesting to note that within the English language most references to meditation or turning inwards include the letter 'I' in their spelling.

Inspiration, intuition, ideas, intelligence, insight, I-con, influence, and illumination are a few examples of this observation. Crying, which is the sudden release of one's tears, is a common emotional response to extreme circumstances. Conditions, be they good or bad, often times may be the trigger. I believe that it is a misjudgment to assume that crying is a weakness in one's character. This release of tears may conceal a person's true inner strength. I find the lack of compassion within an individual to be their true weakness. Long life can be realized through finding the secret of how to replenish and revitalize our energies. This revitalization is achievable through spiritual meditation.

This practice promotes the re-charging of one's batteries, which can defy the aging process. Man's life span is greatly determined by his ability to remain active and healthy. God, our Creator, the giver of life provides all living entities that have the ability to give birth with additional energy. This additional energy is held in reserve to accomplish this goal. Hence, women in general usually out-live their spouses.

One of the keys to finding the true meaning of life and its purpose can be found through Spiritual Meditation. This is a journey within. As I mentioned earlier, I am convinced that lack of understanding of how to commune with our Creator by going inward, has blocked the flow of communication from Spirit. Catholicism is only one of many religions that insist that confession is necessary. It teaches that we must be forgiven of our earthly sins in order to enter Heaven.

Upon confession, our next stop is Purgatory. Upon arriving there, our deeds, which may have been good, bad or indifferent are subject to review. A determination is then made as to whether we go to Hell, or enter into Heaven. The idea of Judgment Day is a man made concept. Our Creator does not judge us; he simply observes. The purpose of life is to experience life itself. We impose are own limitations.

Manmade religion, in my opinion, has created fear in our minds as a means to maintain control over us. I sincerely believe that our greatest power is the power of choice. How we respond to our choices greatly determines what our life in this realm will be like.

I don't believe that Jesus or any other great achiever of the past ever attended a college or a university. Their knowledge and inspiration was divine; their wisdom cannot be gained by merely memorizing passages from religious books. The truth simply is. The practice of spiritual meditation provides us with a means of direct access to the Spirit World of God. The Sun of our solar system is our ultimate source of energy, through light, to all creatures of our universe. The practice of spiritual meditation energizes our Soul, which provides our bodies with vital energy.

Our Soul, which is similar to a battery, must be periodically re-charged and re-energized or otherwise it will eventually run out of energy. Through the practice of spiritual meditation we re-charge our energy source, the Soul. The human body was created to sustain itself for many more years than most people live. By not re-charging and revitalizing our bodies, we diminish the body's natural ability to resist the effects of the aging process.

Our lowered resistance to infections and deceases eventually leads to organ and system failure. Ultimately death of the body ensues. Through the practice of spiritual meditation our bodies unfold. The human body's natural receptors through the Laws of Attraction are replenished with life sustaining energy and vigor. This infusion of vitality contributes to the extension of human life beyond the average lifespan.

CHAPTER 16

My Ultimate Manifest

It rained eleven of the first fourteen days in May of 1998. Although this rainy pattern was a welcomed event for vegetation and farmers, most people in southeastern New England, myself included, found the constant rainy days to be depressing.

In an effort to lift my dampened spirit, I decided to treat myself on Mother's day eve to a performance given by Chaka Khan, who was appearing at the Wolfe's Den Lounge. This lounge was located in the Mohegan Sun Casino in Uncasville, Connecticut, which was located just eight miles north of my home. At the closing of her great performance, I crossed the path of an irresistibly attractive young lady. She fanned herself as she and another young lady passed by. "Are you alright, ma'am," I asked?

"Yes," she replied in a frustrated voice adding, "I'm not old enough to be addressed as ma'am." She and her friend had just entered the lounge as Chaka Khan was singing her last song. In utter frustration, she was trying to fan cigarette smoke as she walked toward an exit.

I had been taught that it was polite to address all women as ma'am. She was offended by the way I addressed her. She felt the implication was that she was an older woman. My attraction to her was immediate so I introduced myself. Her name was Anne and her girlfriend's name was Patricia. They had driven some fifty miles from the city of Providence, Rhode Island to see Chaka Khan perform. By the time they arrived at the lounge, Chaka Khan was nearing the end of her performance.

I tried to make light of their frustration with the evening's events. My comments did little to ease a tense situation. Mesmerized by her beauty, I immediately knew that I had to find a way to see Anne again. I asked her what her occupation was and where she worked. Anne worked as an Account Manager for the American Power Conversion Company, which was located in West Kingston, Rhode Island. American Power Conversion manufactured and sold electrical power serge protection devices, which were used primarily to protect computers from electrical surges.

Her position there often required that she and her peers set up and man displays at trade shows around the country. She owned and resided in a condominium in North Providence, Rhode Island. Her daily commute home was thirty-five miles northeast of where she worked. Upon our meeting that evening, we exchanged work telephone numbers. I left the casino that evening knowing that I had just met someone special.

I called Anne at APC on the following Monday, and asked her out to dinner; she accepted. Our first date would be on

Thursday of the same week. I agreed to pick her up at her place of work at four in the afternoon. We would have dinner at a nearby restaurant of her choosing. After picking her up at her office, she directed me to the Coast Guard House on the beach in Narragansett, Rhode Island.

The Coast Guard House's setting was quite romantic. Once seated, the view of the Atlantic Ocean seemed endless. Our waitress asked if I was driving a BMW. "Yes," was my reply. She suggested that I move it, as it was parked in front of the restaurant's garbage dumpster. "I wouldn't want to see it get damaged," she remarked. I excused myself from the table and moved the car.

As I approached our table, I was stunned to witness Anne buttering my bread. No one had ever done that for me before. I knew then that I was in the company of a very persuasive woman. I couldn't take my eyes off of her; I was smitten. I quickly asked her to tell me all about herself.

Anne was forty-seven years old. She had migrated from the Cape Verde Islands, where she had lived as a young girl. Abandoned by her mother when she was only eight days old, she had been raised by her grandmother, Ana Barros. Her grandfather, Manuel daLomba, whose family originated from the Azores, left Cape Verde and migrated to New Bedford, Massachusetts where he enlisted in the US Navy. Anne was eight years old when he returned to the islands where he lived the last days of his life.

At the age of fourteen, a man who befriended her stepfather raped her. Once captured, he admitted to violating her. He was jailed and brought before the local magistrate.

The magistrate offered him a choice of fifteen years in prison or marriage. Because she was only fourteen, too young to decide her future, her mother was summoned to appear before the magistrate to speak on her behalf. Believing that Anne, having been raped would forever be shunned, her mother pushed for their marriage. These options interfered with the rapist' ultimate plan. The perpetrator had family members who had already migrated to the United States of America. He had planned to follow their footsteps to Pawtucket, Rhode Island, to begin a new life. Her mother believed that although marriage to her rapist would be a horrible choice, she would at least be provided for, securing her future. The decision was made for them to marry. They migrated to the U. S. shortly after the wedding ceremony. Anne's perspective on life, due to her circumstances, was anything but positive. The traumatic experiences she had endured that year was more horrible than any of us could imagine.

The culture and language in Rhode Island was completely different from what she had known. Undaunted by her situation, she vowed to change the dismal circumstances of that year. Her incredible story is chronicled in her autobiography that has been published by iuniverse.com entitled, *Beyond The Shadows: I Was Forced To Marry At Fourteen*.

At the end of our first date, she gave me her home telephone number. The following Sunday morning I dialed the number she had given me. I did not get through because there was no such telephone number listed in the entire Providence area. As there was no listing at all for Anne Baptista, I was beside myself with anger. Had she intentionally given me the wrong telephone number? I immediately felt that she must have had something to hide. Not to be outdone, I needed to confront her face to face. North Providence, Rhode Island, was approximately sixty-five miles northeast of where I lived. I decided to drive there to find her, so I could give her a piece of my mind.

Even if I failed to find her, all would not be lost in my venture to Providence. Ronald Ferguson, an old friend, now lived there. I could always pay him and his wife a visit. With that plan, I set out for North Providence. I arrived in North Providence in about an hour and fifteen minutes. I stopped at a gas station to ask for directions to her street. Two people there gave me different directions. I was thoroughly confused. I instantly recalled passing by the North Providence Police Station. I drove back to the police station to get accurate guidance. Once there an officer advised me that Anne's street was right around the corner. He explained the confusion.

Her street ended at one intersection, and began again three blocks away. I found my way to her building and parked my car. Once I was in the lobby of the condo, I rang the buzzer that listed her name. A voice said, "hello." "Is this the home of Anne Baptista," I asked?

"Yes," she replied.

"Well, this is Greg Branch from Connecticut."

She rang me in. Her condo was located on the second floor, number 209. I knocked on the door. Her facial expression upon opening the door was one of shock. She invited me in and offered me a seat. Once seated, I immediately noticed and mentioned that she and I had the very same sofa and loveseat. I had not seen that pattern of upholstery anywhere else. Her condo seemed warm and inviting. Not to change the subject, I voiced my anger, in her giving me the wrong phone number. She apologized for the confusion, and explained that she had just changed her telephone number. Giving me the wrong number had been purely unintentional. Since I had not been invited there, I felt rather uncomfortable. I left shortly after I arrived.

From the time of my initial visit to Anne's condo, I had to fight off my desire to be in her presence. The following Wednesday was a day off from work for me, so I decided to use that time to clean my basement. This would occupy my mind and contain my overwhelming thoughts of being in Anne's company.

While I was in my basement, I uncovered an old wall safe that I had purchased it at a yard sale two years before. My plan was to store valuables in it. With its exterior dimensions of two ft. by two ft., steel construction, weighing approximately six hundred pounds, I felt it would be ideal for my purpose. Using its large numerical dial, I could enter the combination to gain entry. A large steel wheel, similar to the kind you'd find on a hatch aboard a ship, opened the safe. Once opened, however, its interior space was rather small. It was too small in fact for important documents. Because of its age and unique appearance, I felt it would serve as a good conversation piece. I had its four-digit combination written on a 3x5 card. I had only unlocked it once before, on the day I bought it. On this day, two years later, it took three tries before I was successful in opening it.

Because of its extreme weight, it still sat on the dolly that came with it. After opening it for the first time, I pushed it back into the corner of my basement. Suddenly, I was interrupted by the telephone. Anne, my new heartthrob, was on the other end of the telephone. I was excited; it was the very first time she had called me since we met. During that conversation, I asked her, "when is your birthday?"

"August sixth, I was born in 1952", she remarked.

I was stunned to realize that her birth date 08/06/52 was also the numerical combination to my safe. I immediately remembered that we had the same patterns in our living room furniture. In addition to that, she had two live parakeets in her condo, while I had two hand painted wooden parakeets as plant ornaments in my living room. I should also mention that the last two digits in the year of Anne's birth equaled my age. The last two digits in the year of my birth equaled her age.

Could our meeting have been more than a casual one? I added this unlikely coincidence to the fact that my attraction to her was overwhelming. I knew immediately that Anne was indeed the woman prophesied by Spirit through Carl Hewitt. Over the next six months we spent every weekend together. The distance between our homes was 65 miles. Although that was not a great distance, we decided to try out living together. Eight months later Anne asked for my hand in marriage. Although I was completely surprised, I accepted her proposal without any hesitation. On July 5, 1999 we got married. Our joyous wedding ceremony was held at the Regatta Club on Goat Island in Newport, Rhode Island. Our immediate family members made up the wedding party, with four of our daughters serving as Anne's bridesmaids. Kathleen Guillen, Anne's eldest daughter served as the maid of honor. The groomsmen consisted of my three brothers and a cousin, Everett G. Simonds, who resided in Stonington, Connecticut. At Anne's request, my father agreed to give her away, as she had only seen her biological father once in her life. That meeting occurred back at her childhood home in the Cape Verde Islands. Her father was a native of Senegal, which is a nation located on the Continent of Africa. My sister Tamara, who lived in Los Angeles, California, opened the ceremony with a poem. Carl Hewitt, who was also an ordained spiritual minister, presided over our wedding. He announced at the wedding reception that Anne and I would someday make great contributions to the betterment of mankind. We, to this day, cannot imagine what he meant by that statement. I'm sure that time will eventually determine the validity of such a lofty prediction.

In that same year, Spirit again used Carl Hewitt to ask if I had ever considered writing. My reply was abruptly, "no."

Spirit predicted that I would be driven to write sometime in the future. I was cautioned against trying to quell this desire. "Don't fight this urge," I was told, "as it will be of a spiritual nature." Because I'm not a writer, I am amazed and overwhelmed with my desire to write this book. I started this writing on the first anniversary of my mother's passing. She and I were very close. Many passages in this book have come to me as a whisper in her voice.

Chapter 17

▼

Our New Home

Seven months after Anne and I were married, we sold the home I owned in Oakdale, Connecticut. Again in the year 2000, Spirit said that I would purchase a piece of land. A river would serve as one of its' boundaries and the riverbanks would be overgrown with mountain laurel. The land would be laden with dense vegetation and be situated close to a major interstate highway.

That same year Anne and I decided to purchase a home that would be large enough to accommodate my parents. We did not want them to spend their remaining years in a convalescent home. We searched for weeks but did not find any existing homes that met our needs. We then made the decision to find land and build a home according to our needs. We decided that purchasing land midway between New London, Connecticut, where I worked and Providence, Rhode Island, where Anne worked, would be the ideal location. We sought out and found a real estate agent who was familiar with that area. She directed us to a parcel of land that was for sale in the town of Hopkinton, Rhode Island. It was located twenty-two miles from where I worked and thirty-seven miles from where Anne worked. The property, which measured 3.8 acres, was situated on the Wood River. It had a breathtaking view that included a dam with a waterfall.

The existing house on the property had previously been condemned. Town building codes required it to be demolished. In spite of the added expense of having the house removed, Anne and I immediately fell in love with the property. We put a retainer on it, which gave us first right of refusal. The State of Rhode Island's Department of Environmental Management required that this property be tested for proper water drainage. The test results would not be available to us for sixty days. Anne and I used that time to acquaint ourselves' with the property; we had already taken mental ownership of it.

The final results of the water drainage test however, revealed that the property had very poor water drainage. New home construction would require a very expensive engineered septic system. This added expense in addition to the cost of the property, simply put the purchase beyond our means. Feeling totally frustrated by the circumstances, we decided to walk away. Knowing that we could not afford that property left us depressed. I doubted that we would ever find another piece of land we'd like as much. However, we had made up our minds that we wanted to live in that area. A local surveyor provided us with a list of available parcels of land. During one of our searches, I was attracted to a small red building. The sign on it read, Wood

River Golf. As I entered the building I was greeted by, the proprietor, Katie Thompson. She and her husband, Wes Thompson, were converting their farmland into a golf course. Since the local news media had just reported seeing a large bear in that area, Anne and I decided to stop and ask for directions. I asked Katie if she knew the location of the land I was searching for.

Katie wasn't sure but she suspected that the land I was in search of was located next to their property. She inquired as to what my plans were for the land. I indicated that my wife and I wanted to build a home. She casually mentioned that if we didn't find what we were looking for, we might consider looking at a piece of property they owned in the next town of Richmond, Rhode Island. They had just decided to list their property for sale with a local real estate agent.

After discussing the offer with Anne, we decided to look at their available land. I set up an appointment with Wes Thompson to walk the property on the following Friday. I met Wes at their golf course and rode with him to the property which was not far way. Since Wes Thompson had not walked the property in many years, he was not quite sure of its boundaries. Realizing this, he had already made arrangements to have the land surveyed. The property was beautiful; I immediately fell in love with it. I was confident that the home Anne and I planned to build would sit perfectly on it.

My excitement at the prospect of buying the property was limited by the strong possibility that Anne and I would not be able to afford it. Wes did not give me his asking price for the land at that showing; he suggested that I show the property to Anne first. If she liked it, we could then negotiate. Two days later, Anne and I walked the property. Because the property was densely wooded and isolated, Anne had reservations about our purchasing it; that however, was her only reservation about it. She loved it.

We contacted Wes and Katie Thomson to arrange for a meeting to discuss the particulars of the purchase. They invited us to meet them that same day at their golf course. Wes had indicated during our first meeting that he would do everything within his power to make the property affordable to us. Wes did, in fact, keep his word. On a handshake, we closed the deal. Ninety days later, we closed on the sale of the property. Only after the closing, did Anne and I realize the significance of our purchase.

The property also bordered the Wood River. The riverbanks were covered with mountain laurel. The property was part of a forest which had never been built on. Once again, a Spirit prophecy had become a reality. We took our time when it came to choosing a building contractor. We finally chose Mr. Pete Peloquin. He not only had a great reputation as a builder, but he also resided in the nearby town of Ashaway, Rhode Island. He worked tirelessly with our banker to keep the expense of building our dream home within our budget.

Because I had Fridays off, I visited the property on those days. On one of those visits, I lost my sunglasses and doubted that I'd ever see them again. I realized that finding them would be like trying to find a needle in a haystack. A week later, while walking the property, I almost stepped on them. Since I never expected to find them, I considered that occurrence to be a good omen. From that moment on, I was convinced that our purchase had been blessed. During one of those Friday visits, I noticed that a huge tree had fallen as a result of a recent storm. I immediately made the decision to use its location as the footprint for our new home. Construction of our new home began in September 2001.

Chapter 18

A Celebration for Mom

In November that same year, I sought out Carl Hewitt for spiritual advice with the building process. During that reading, Spirit made me aware that my father's heart was failing; Spirit did not give him much more time to live. Spirit assured me that my father would see and be in our new home when it was completed. Shortly after that reading, my father underwent surgery to have a defibrillator attached to his heart. The procedure was successful; he remained in the hospital for two weeks to recover.

One week after my father's surgery, my mother was admitted to the same hospital with medical problems of her own. Once admitted, she was given antibiotics intravenously to rid her body of a UTI infection. Both parents remained in the hospital for the next two weeks. My siblings and I hired caregivers to assist our parents in their home as we nervously awaited our new homes' completion.

In preparation for the move to our new house, Anne and I sold the condo that we lived in North Providence. Within one week in May 2002, we had two closings and moved into our new home. We aptly named our new property, "Branch Haven"; it was perfect for us. We instantly felt comfortable in our new home. We knew however, we'd have to leave it, and go to work, to pay for it.

Shortly after we moved in, my parents came to visit. Anne and I were proud and excited about them moving in. Anne, who was a fabulous cook, prepared a dinner that was fitting for the 'king and queen' of our family. Over dinner we asked, "When can we start moving you guys in?" They weren't sure. "We'll let you know," was their reply. Anne and I had made all the necessary arrangements. A caregiver would come to the house to cater to their needs during the weekdays while Anne and I worked. We would spend the evenings and all our weekends together. Anne and I designed our new home so that my parents could live on the first floor. My mother who had Multiple Sclerosis was confined to a wheelchair. Living on the first level of the home would make her getting around less of a challenge. We overlooked no details in designing our new home to accommodate my parents.

During a previous spiritual reading, it was predicted that Anne and I would host a joyous celebration in our new home. I was told that there would be large tents set in the yard with a number of people in attendance, both friends and family. This gathering would take place on a summer day resembling a wedding. There would be music and lots of food to enjoy. Since Anne and I were only focused on getting settled in our new home, I gave this prediction little thought. After their third visit to our new home, my parents announced to us that they would not be moving in. To say the least, Anne and I were devastated by my parent's decision. We believed that they would simply require additional convincing. They however, were overly concerned that their moving in would be a burden on us. We immediately began a campaign to overturn their initial decision. We enlisted the help and influence of family members and their closest friends. "We'll think it over," they'd say. Patience is a virtue; conversely we believed they would change their minds. We were confident that they would eventually see things our way. Each time they came to visit, we would bring up the subject with caution. We did not want to apply too much pressure.

My youngest brother and sister flew in from California to spend Mother's Day with us. It was at that time that we decided to plan a surprise birthday party for mother. Planning such an event, while keeping it a secret was quite a challenge. We decided to have the party on the Saturday before her birthday. My mother's birthday, which was on July twenty-second, fell on a weekday. Since my mother's family was so large, her birthday party would serve as a family reunion as well. My aunt, Edna Vinters, who was a travel agent and one of my uncles, Julius Pertillar, volunteered to get word of the event out to family members. My father put the word out to my mother's closest friends. My aunt Edna made all the arrangements to secure a bus to transport members of the family. We rented a large tent, tables, chairs, a Porta Potty, and a large grill for the occasion. A party rental agency delivered and set up these items on the morning of the party. What a glorious affair it was; the weather was ideal. It was sunny with temperatures in the mid eighties.

We prearranged the arrival time of relatives and friends. A group of eight, which included my daughter, and my siblings with their friends, flew in from Los Angeles. My niece and nephew, Cherise and Mikell Branch, accompanied them. Once the bus arrived, it was emptied and hidden out of sight. All the guests hid behind our home so they could not to be seen. Once my parents arrived, we navigated my mother through the house and onto the back deck.

"Surprise", everyone shouted. I thought my mother was going into shock. She was literally stunned and without words. Tears of joy and happiness ran down her cheeks. It was a joyous occasion for all. This celebration was quite fitting as my mother, in her gracious manner had been an inspiration to so many people. She had received numerous civic awards and was honored for her enduring and unwavering contributions to youth. She continuously encouraged them to focus on education. She never allowed the challenges of Multiple Sclerosis to deter her from continuing on with her life. Her zest for life and her positive energy was infectious. Reverend Jesse Jackson, upon meeting her in a Hartford hospital, publically applauded the inspiration her life had been to so many. He was convinced that her presence was a rare gift from God.

DOMINION

Man was created by God to have dominion over the face of the earth
Not dominion over other humans
Mankind's choice to conquer and enslave nations and its inhabitants
Was never God's intention for us
"Due unto others as you would have them due unto you
"Love thy neighbors as thy self"
Was God's true intention for mankind

Chapter 19

My Parents' Passing

Mankind's greatest power is the power of choice. Because we are born into this life with amnesia, we have no memory of previous lives. In the Spirit world, we still possess the power of choice and choose the host parents of our next incarnation. The DNA of our host parents determines most of our physical characteristics. My choice in choosing my parents as host during this life was a wise one; I could not have chosen better parents. My parents were simply my superheroes; they provided me with infinite life experiences. I will forever be indebted to them. My parents instilled in my siblings and I two commandments to live by: first, "Honor Thy Neighbor As Thy Self"; second, "Do Unto Others, As You Would Have Them Do Unto You."

On May 23, 2003 my great father passed from this earthly plane, succumbing to congestive heart failure. I will never recover from his loss; memories of him are part of my daily thoughts. His passing left a void in our family that words alone could never convey. Almost two thousand people paid their final respects at my fathers wake. The town of Bloomfield's Police Department led my father's funeral procession from the funeral home to the cemetery to minimize traffic congestion. The great number of people present was like a sea of humanity. The funeral procession covered almost an entire city block.

With the passing of my father, my siblings and I focused on the care and well being of our mother. My parents had been married for fifty-seven years; they were inseparable. I could count on one hand the number of times they were apart. Now that my father had passed on, concern for my mother's state of mind became our utmost priority. My mother did not mourn outwardly for very long. My siblings stayed with her for approximately two weeks after dad's burial.

Now that Dad was gone, we all assumed that Mom would finally agree to live with us. She however, was more comfortable in her own home. She cherished her independence and lived for the continued interaction with her students. She was also the oldest of seven sisters and six brothers that were still living. She relied heavily on her network of friends, and her close affiliation with the senior citizen's center in her town. The idea of not being there to share a game of bingo or penuckle with friends was out of the question. She continued to be instrumental in keeping family members acquainted. My mother remained defiant about moving out of the home in which she and my father had shared so many memories. My parents moved to Bloomfield, Connecticut, which was a suburb of the city of Hartford, in 1954. They were both born and raised in that city.

Suburban Bloomfield was not as rural as Richmond, Rhode Island. My mother viewed the transition to be cultural shock. Although Anne and I encouraged my mother to live with us, we respected her final decision to stay the course, and to live out her remaining days in her own home. She would often have Luzy Galarza, a friend and a skilled caregiver drive her out to our home to spend Sunday afternoons. We celebrated her seventy-eighth birthday at our place. Her aunt Vester, two of her sisters, Emily and Virginia and a host of others accompanied her for the party. We had a great day together. In addition to being stricken with Multiple Sclerosis, my mother's vision was limited by the progression of glaucoma. Control of this condition required her to have eye drops daily. As her vision was limited, she would always leave for home before sunset. She never accepted our offers to stay overnight.

Hoping that she might eventually agree to live with us, we continuously interviewed perspective local caregivers. That person would have to cater to my mother's needs while providing daytime companionship. Thanks to my mother's siblings, friends, and her temporary caregivers, she was never left alone.

By June of 2004, it was apparent that my mother would need to have a responsible caregiver move into her home. Because she was already a foster mother to a teenage girl, as well as a single parent to her own two daughters, Luzy was unable to move in with my mother as we would have preferred.

Even though my mother's resistance to infection had become low, she continued to strive forward with life in spite of the absence of my father. Her strength and resiliency wavered as she contracted numerous urinary track infections. These infections would leave her disoriented, since her nervous system was already compromised due to her Multiple Sclerosis. Those UTI infections put her in a delusional state of mind. Treatment with antibiotics intravenously usually required her to spend numerous days in a nearby hospital. Unfortunately, my mother's loved ones and I, got to know the medical staff at the local hospital quite well.

My mother and I continued our search for a live-in caregiver. We listed our search in the local newspaper and immediately received numerous phone inquiries. We arranged for personal interviews to be held on Fridays when I spent the day with her. We interviewed three applicants on the very first day of interviews. Ms. Tamara East was one of the first applicants. She provided us with an impressive list of recommendations. Mother liked her instantly. I liked her as well, but I had reservations concerning her dependability and immediate intentions. Even though she was only twenty-five years old, Tamara assured us that she was quite settled and that she was looking to find a live-in arrangement. She had earned an associate's degree in nursing. Her experience and love for care giving was quite apparent. Her long-term goal was to acquire a BA in tourism. She planned to enroll with an on line university to complete the required courses.

Tamara was a native of Jamaica. After receiving a degree in tourism, she intended to return to her native home to work in that field. In spite of Tamara's youth, she appeared to be very mature. Although my mother and I felt obligated to interview other applicants, we were hopeful that she would still be available at the end of our interviewing process. Because of her youth, we remained cautious about her immediate goals and continued to interview other perspective applicants. One week later we hired her; she moved in the very same day. Angels must have sent her to us.

Her professionalism left nothing to be desired. She and my mother related to one another as if they had known each other for years. Her ability to communicate with my mother's healthcare professionals, as well as with the family, was a breath of fresh air. The bond between she and my mother became so strong, at times I had to insist that she take a day off to restore and recharge her own energies. Her presence gave the family peace of mind we had not been accustomed to.

My siblings flew in from Los Angeles just before Thanksgiving of 2004. Our mother had just returned home from another stay in the hospital. It was agreed by all of us, including my lovely wife Anne, that we should celebrate Thanksgiving at Mom's place. The day had special meaning to all of us because the entire family was together once again.

By the end of that summer, it was apparent that my mother had become too week to resume her passion of working with fourth graders at the Metacomet Elementary School. That reality broke my mother's will to carry on. She had devoted the last thirty-eight years of her life to teaching and interacting with the youth in her community. She always insisted that the give and take exchange she experienced with them, provided her with more uplifting than any of her medical prescriptions. The possibility that she might be able to return to the classroom provided her with remarkable drive and persistence to carry on. My mother's doctors however, discouraged her from returning to the classroom. With that decision my mother, I believe, gave up on her will to live. Again, she had to be admitted to the hospital to receive antibiotics to ward off yet another infection. Christmas was only a few days away. My brother Randy and his partner, Belinda, flew in from Los Angeles to share the holiday with us. It was not a joyous occasion. Due to our mother's exhaustion; she slept throughout the holiday.

She did regain consciousness on the day after Christmas. She was however, quite week and could barely speak. Over the weeks following Christmas, my mother struggled to remain conscious. On February 7, 2005, she gave up her struggle to live and left this dimension. She was finally free from earthly burdens. Her life, her energy, and her light were transformed as she was transported to a higher dimension. No one will ever fill the void she left behind. Her passing was a great loss of a graceful, humble, loving soul.

The challenges she overcame during her lifetime served as a shining example to all that the power of the mind, with reverence to God, our Creator, makes all things possible. The passing of my mother has left me in agony. Our family take comfort in knowing that she is now finally free of any pain and is reunited with her long time partner, our father. I will forever be grateful for having them as my parents.

They were married for fifty-seven years. My mother remained strong and positive about life even after my dad passed on. Because of Spirit's prediction, my mother's passing was not a complete surprise to me. Spirit revealed to me that she secretly had a death wish to leave this existence and to be re-united with my father. My mother passed on six hundred and twenty-five days after my father did. The wake for my mother was so large that the area surrounding the funeral home was virtually paralyzed. It was estimated that over five thousand people paid their final respects to her. Only the immediate family was allowed to witness her burial at the cemetery. The number of lives she impacted will never be known.

Chapter 20

▼

Carl Hewitt's Passing

On January 26, 2005, twelve days before my mother's passing, I lost my dear friend, Carl Hewitt. Carl had moved to Charleston, South Carolina the year before. Having suffered a stroke, daily migraine headaches left him almost paralyzed with pain. He decided that Charleston's warmer climate would make his condition less afflicting. Medical experts had determined that a tumor in his brain, although benign, was the reason for his paralyzing headaches. Removing the tumor was going to be necessary. Carl unfortunately, did not survive the surgery. He gave up his physical body and passed on to a higher dimension. During his lifetime, his reputation as a gifted spiritual medium spread to many areas of the world. He gave readings to clients from as far away as Hong Kong and Ghana. He was once sought out and gave a spiritual reading for the oil minister of Saudi Arabia.

Mr. Sydney Swartz of Hackensack, New Jersey, was Carl's lifelong friend and companion. He and Carl had not only traveled the world together, they also had co-authored two books on the Gifts of the Spirit. The first book was entitled, *My First Encounter With An Angel,* the second was entitled, *Crossovers.* Sydney, who is also a gifted person in his own right, continues to lead the church that Carl founded. Sydney still works full-time for the Tenakill Middle School located in Closter, New Jersey. He has worked there for many years as the school librarian.

My relationship with Carl evolved over the years and we became very special friends. We spent time together beyond the realm of spiritual matters. Once during the construction of our new home, he had the opportunity to visit the site. At that time he assured me that our contractor was a knowledgeable and skilled builder. After our home was completed he was invited for a visit along with friends and family. It was then that he told us that our home was blessed and that the Spirits were keeping us safe.

Knowing him forever changed my relationship with all living things. Through my unique relationship with Carl Hewitt, I became educated and enlightened in the essence of life: past, present, and future. He often openly announced that I was the brother he never had. It was indeed an honor to know him. Through him, I learned the importance and special significance of all life, both seen and unseen. I learned that all life has a pulse and possesses energy. He taught me that energy cannot be destroyed; it can and does take on different forms. Nature holds the foundation by which all life thrives. God, our Creator, through nature provides us with living examples of his majesty.

God has provided mankind with a direct means of attuning ourselves in alignment with his Kingdom. It is not necessary to go to a designated place to worship and receive the benefits of His unseen Kingdom. Multitudes have perished at the hands of one another because they lack the understanding of Spirit.

Chapter 21

The Advantages of Spiritual Meditation

The sun of our solar system is the primary source of light in our universe. The sun not only provides light but it also provides life to all living things. The plant kingdom thrives by absorbing light from the sun and converting it into energy; this process is known as photosynthesis. Mankind, in general, only fully appreciates this process during the change of the seasons. Most perennials of the plant kingdom recharge themselves by going dormant during the colder months of the year. During the winter months, many of these plants loose their foliage and redirect their energies to conserve and restore themselves by turning inward. Because they are in harmony with nature's seasonal change, they often outlive humans.

Mankind has been reactive in respect and appreciation for the wonders of nature and the preservation of our planet. Greed, power, and ignorance are seeds that have spawned a general malaise in the quality of life for far too many. Our youth are taught that morality is un-important. Our children are programmed at very young ages that *Mutant Ninja Turtles* are examples of positive role models, and that we should *Be Like Mike.* Too often Hollywood movie producers portray blood and guts sagas with unhallowed glory. Mutual respect and appreciation for nature holds the real key to spiritual illumination. Mankind derives light from the sun through the Soul. An invisible golden thread exists between all living beings of our dimension to the Spirit world. This invisible golden thread extends upward from the top of our heads into infinity. Through this invisible thread, we are energized from Spirit by the sun of our solar system. This invisible golden chord is broken or severed at the moment of death. The Soul instantaneously leaves the body as life continues in an unseen or spiritual form. This transition is so immediate that often times one does not realize that they have physically passed over. This transition happens without interruption as we seemingly walk out of the physical room of life, and enter the spiritual room of life.

Through meditation we consciously slow down our heartbeat. This reduces stress on the body's systems and organs. Spiritual Meditation allows for the regeneration of energy necessary to sustain life. Depletion of this energy leads to the body's ultimate failure, death.

Here is a testimony of a woman whom I met at a spiritual retreat in Yelm, Washington in 1997. She credited the practice of daily spiritual meditation with reversing the aging process of her body; this woman was in her late sixties. She had gone through the natural change of life during her late fifties. She believed that the practice of spiritual meditation had caused her reproductive organs to become fertile again. After many months of practicing spiritual meditation, she resumed having a monthly menstruation. She hadn't experienced menstruation in at least ten years.

I'm not, however, suggesting that daily meditation will defy and in some cases reverse the natural aging process. The invigorating affects of this practice will vary with each individual. Our heredity in large measure determines the physical attributes of all of us. Focused spiritual meditation will only contribute to keeping us vital.

DENIAL

Denial ... not the river Nile
Flows against the current of the river of spiritual knowledge
Manmade religion can't seem to envision
The wisdom of looking to nature & learning to go within
From there the answers and guidance we seek is displayed
before us
All that glitters is not gold
Find the light within your soul, for knowledge untold
Find your light ... it will make all things right
Find your light ... be right

Chapter 22

▼

The Rhythm of Life

I should make the reader aware that I'm open to and believe that there is more than one manner by which we might receive inspiration through creation. My lovely wife, Anne, talks openly to the plants and flowers in her gardens. This practice may seem to be strange to many; however, I must say that the response to her conversations has provided remarkable results. We were told that because our property was so sandy, little vegetation would survive without spreading topsoil. We took our chances without investing in topsoil. The maturity and beauty of her gardens has left our friends and neighbors alike in awe. She genuinely believes that their majestic presence is a direct response to her verbal encouragement. Very few people consider and accept the possibility that nature has the ability to respond to vibrations, be they positive or negative.

Again, this is an example of how mankind's inflated ego overlooks the fact that other kingdoms possess the ability to communicate. I think that it is worth noting that the animals located in the area of Indonesia's most recent tsunami seemed to have been forewarned of impending danger. Only the animals that could not get to higher ground were lost.

Worship of material things in life without reverence to God leaves one open to pain and agony in life. This unfortunate result may be experienced directly or indirectly through self, as well as loved ones.

Our culture, which has become suspect in its belief systems, has promoted a climate of violence, mistrust, and negativity towards one another. Respect for life is at an all time low. Shoot first, ask questions later, seems to be the acceptable practice. My wife has a very good philosophy; she believes that we should wait twenty-four hours before responding to confrontation. Usually within that period, cooler heads will have prevailed, as the heat of that moment will have passed. This is a healthy attitude that we all should apply when dealing with others. Learning to go within, the practice of spiritual meditation can be helpful in dealing with many challenges in our daily lives. This is especially true in dealing with the stresses of negative and often unforeseen situations. My wife and I have three bronze statues of monkeys in the foyer of our home. They serve as constant reminders: Speak No Evil, Hear No Evil, and See No Evil. The practice of spiritual meditation promotes calmness in the midst of turmoil. I credit the practice of spiritual meditation, along with the love and support of my wife, with helping me to get through many of my own traumatic situations.

The belief that acknowledgement of our Creator through worship alone will sustain life, and provide us with entry into the Hereafter is futile. The animal kingdom exists in harmony with nature. Many animals hibernate during the winter months. This form of meditation allows them to recharge and restore their energies. Many species of birds migrate closer to the equator during colder months. There, they are able to conserve and restore their energies.

Chapter 23

Consider This

Mankind is still devoted to belief in mainstream religion. He fails to recognize the necessity of turning inward, through spiritual meditation, to replenish life sustaining vital energy. We are all born with a soft spot at the top of our skulls; this soft spot is the void between the two halves of the skull. Vital force or energy from our Creator enters the human body through this void. As our bodies develop, the two halves of our skull fuse together.

This energy resides in and is known as the Soul. The Soul distributes energy throughout our body, as it is needed. The human body was designed by God to support life well in excess of a hundred years. Failure to re-energize one's Soul accounts for the reason why the average human beings' lifespan is significantly shorter. Aside from mankind, all the other living species of our planet take steps to recharge their bodies. Our lack of understanding of the Gifts of the Spirit leads to fatal consequences in the end.

I am convinced that mainstream religious leaders will discourage dialog among their followers regarding the contents of this book. They might consider my point of view to be a threat to their ideology. Earlier in this book, I indicated that there were over eleven hundred different religions throughout the world. Although that might sound like an exaggeration, it is not. Our world population currently exceeds six billion people practicing over eleven hundred different religions. Many modern societies find my belief in reincarnation to be unrealistic. My wife, Anne and I, have a small brass plate mounted near the doorbell at the front door of our home. Inscribed on this plate is the following saying: "We thank you in advance for leaving your ego outside." We believe that these words are self-explanatory. We also believe that, actions speak louder than words. Inviting those you hold dear into your home to break bread is the ultimate show of friendship.

Over my lifetime I have been fortunate to cross the paths of many people who were independent thinkers. It comes as no surprise to me that many of the world's most influential people, both past and present, were and are, humble about their achievements and contributions to the betterment of mankind. Individualistic thought tends to attract spiritual insight and intellectual illumination.

I'm convinced that to find the Kingdom of God, one must learn to go within. Learning the secret of calming one's self fosters good will. Anger can be calmed through spiritual pursuit.

The drive and desire for money and what having it will provide, is a manmade addition. God's rewards are not material.

Our Creator in his omnipotence has provided us with the opportunity to become reborn. The Law of Attraction makes this possible.

Although I may never acquire great financial wealth, I have enjoyed life's abundance. I have learned how to manifest what I desire through the practice of Consciousness and Energy. My greatest manifestation to date has been to realize and to share a life with my lovely wife, Anne. She, not me, comes first. Through her, I have learned one of life's greatest lessons: One must learn to give first in order to receive. I've come to realize that unfathomable joy awaits anyone who learns to "put someone else first" in their lives. Whether it is for an individual, a group, a cause, or a people, our gratitude never fails to go without notice, respect, and appreciation in the Spirit world. "All things are possible to he who believes." Again, universal law applies. Through the Laws of Attraction what we desire can be manifested and become real. This knowledge allows us to position ourselves to receive that which we focus on the most.

The pyramids of ancient Egypt are just one of many wonders of our world constructed with the use of a technology, which exceeds the modern world's most advanced abilities. These marvels and other great structures of the world were constructed with spiritual assistance. If 'knowledge is power,' then where did this knowledge come from? I subscribe to the theory of spiritual intervention.

My inspiration to write this book was prophesized through Carl Hewitt many years before I actually started it; the exact date of this prophecy escapes me. During that same reading, it was suggested that my purpose in this life would be to 'heal the minds' of those whose path I cross. I hope that this book opens the minds of all who take the time to read it.

Legend has it that Johnny Appleseed planted apple seeds throughout North America. It is my hope to sow seeds of spiritual enlightenment. Margie Coleman, an entertainer from Los Angeles once said, "Each One Teach One, and Everyone Will Learn." Communication with God the Creator, although it may be universally available to us all, is intended to be personal. My point of view is simply: AS I SEE IT. On this day, Father's Day, I believe that while we honor our fathers, we should not forget to honor God, the Father of all living things.

I'm quite sure that most of us are familiar with the expression: 'if you don't use it, you'll loose it. Mankind has gotten away from the practice of spiritual meditation. Wisdom and knowledge from unseen dimensions is still available to us. The same principles apply with spiritual influence. For this reason, the practice of Consciousness and Energy (C&E) as it is known by students of this understanding as, 'The Work.'

This practice of (C&E) facilitates the opening up of the seven seals of the body. It begins at the groin, and leads upward to the top of the skull. Once there, we enter a state of consciousness known as the 'Infinite Unknown.' There, all things are revealed. It is imperative that mankind resorts back to the practice of spiritual meditation. This practice not only benefits us on an individual basis, but collectively it improves mankind's condition and relationship to our environment, the planet earth.

The Laws of Attraction are a constant force of influence in our world. Disconnection of spiritual thought has led to plagues, disease, violence, and pestilence, along with the depletion of many of our natural resources. Our world is in utter chaos. Whether you agree with my point of view or not, is not really the issue. I am simply a messenger. As I stated earlier, I believe in reincarnation. We repeat life in the physical world until we learn our purpose. My purpose is to help make known, 'The unknown.' This is my gift from Spirit; I implore you to consider this message. It is not too late to reverse our current state of affairs. More is lost by 'indecision than by wrong decisions.' The greatest thing that I have ever learned is that I still have a lot to learn. For those of you who read the bible, I remind you that it is written in First Corinthians 12:1, "I will not have you ignorant of the Gifts of the Spirit."

Mankind's desire to be accepted by 'God' is boundless. Our universe is timeless. Learning how to manifest through the knowledge of the Gifts of the Spirit … PRICELESS.

SO BE IT

Back Page Biography

The author takes the reader on a spiritual journey. His journey begins with the first encounter with a medium named Carl Hewitt. In the book he chronicles how his awareness and understanding of the Gifts of Spirit affected his life. Belief in the Baptist way of life was a mainstay in his family. At the age of fourteen, he was initiated into the Baptist Religion by baptism. At the age of twenty-one, while serving in the Navy during the Viet Nam war, he received a letter from his church. It was not a letter of encouragement and support, but rather a reminder of overdue tithes. That letter forever changed his point of view of his church's relationship with God.

Gregory L. Branch holds a degree in psychology, has practiced and studied the benefits of spiritual meditation over 30 years. The author gives a candid viewpoint of a spiritual world unknown to most. AS I SEE IT clearly states his uncommon and unpopular position concerning mankind's relationship with God through religion. The content of this book will surely create much controversy and dialog on this subject. The words will provide insight and the benefits of spiritual meditation.

This awareness allows us to commune with those of the Spirit world any time and any place. It is not intended to discourage the reader from practicing the religion of their choice. But rather to hopefully inspire the reader to become better acquainted with spiritual communication. The author sincerely believes that this knowledge, when practiced consistently will enhance their religious experience.

Footprints

One night a man had a dream. He dreamed he was walking along the beach with the Lord. Across the sky flashed scenes from his life. For each scene, he noticed two sets of footprints in the sand; one belonged to him, and the other belonged to the Lord.

When the last scene of his life flashed before him, he looked back at footprints in the sand. He noticed that many times along the path of his life there was only one set of footprints. He also noticed that it happened at the very lowest and saddest times in his life.

This really bothered him and he questioned the Lord about it. "Lord, you said that once I decided to follow you, you'd walk with me all the way. But I have noticed that during the most troublesome times in my life, there's only one set of footprints. I don't understand why when I needed you most you would leave me."

The Lord replied, "My precious, precious child, I love you and would never leave you. During your times of trail and suffering, when you see only one set of footprints, it was then that I carried you."

This poem hangs in my office—its author is unknown to me

978-0-595-44270-6
0-595-44270-6